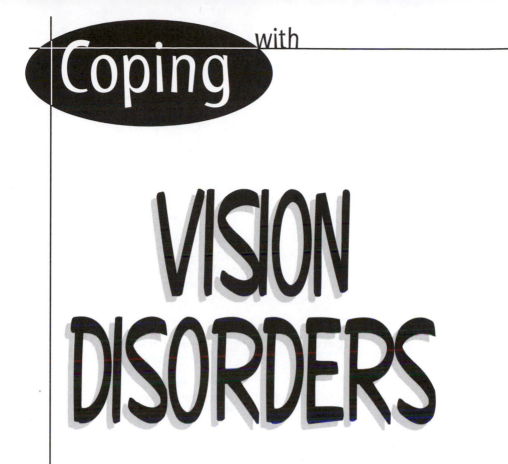

Coping with

VISION DISORDERS

Debbie Stanley

The Rosen Publishing Group, Inc.
New York

Published in 2001 by The Rosen Publishing Group, Inc.
29 East 21st Street, New York, NY 10010

First Edition

Cover photo © Cindy Reiman

Library of Congress Cataloging-in-Publication Data

Stanley, Debbie.
  Coping with vision disorders / by Debbie Stanley. — 1st ed.
      p.   cm.
Includes bibliographical references (p.   ).
  ISBN 0-8239-3198-6
  1. Vision disorders—Juvenile literature. [1. Vision disorders.]
I. Title.
  RE52 .S728 2000
  617.7—dc21
                                                    00-009605

Manufactured in the United States of America

About the Author

Debbie Stanley has a bachelor's degree in journalism and a master's in industrial/organizational psychology.

Contents

Introduction: The World as You See It

If you have impaired vision, whether it's nearsightedness or low vision, you are part of the estimated 50 in 1,000 American children who have a serious eye disorder. You may even be one in twelve of those fifty who require some form of special education because of it.

Also, if you have impaired vision, you have learned not to take your sense of sight for granted. You may have also learned that people who are lucky enough to have problem-free vision often do take it for granted. In their blissful ignorance to your less-than-perfect view of life, they may say or do insensitive things that serve only to make you feel more different, more isolated, angry, sad, or misunderstood.

The goal of this book is to help you learn about vision disorders and the impact they can have on a person's life. If you are visually impaired yourself, this book offers you insight into the facts of your condition as well as the feelings that you might experience as a result of it. If you are a friend or family member of a visually impaired person, this book will enlighten you to the problems faced by visually impaired people and will show you ways that you can help.

We begin in chapters 1 through 3 with an overview of many of the conditions that can lead to vision impairment or blindness. There are a great number of things that can

1

endanger or steal your sight. But since this book is intended to help you cope with a problem you already have, there is less emphasis on prevention and more on providing information about these conditions, including ways to slow their progress or prevent further complications, if possible.

There are treatment options available to correct vision impairments, including many relatively new procedures. These options, and the questions you should ask yourself about them, are discussed in chapters 4 and 5.

Chapter 6 presents some insight into the emotional issues surrounding vision impairment. The stereotypes of blind people as saintly, helpless, angry, or bitter are just that—stereotypes—and are not accurate representations of all blind people. People react in different ways to vision impairment, and their attitudes toward it will likely change over time. The goal of this chapter is to help you understand what you or a friend might be feeling as a visually impaired person.

Chapter 7 offers some tools and resources for dealing with vision impairment. There are people and products available that can make a significant difference in how well you are able to utilize your sight. In many cases, these resources can restore a person's active lifestyle or his or her ability to work or attend school. When adapting to a loss of vision, one of the most important considerations is safety. You'll find information on that topic in chapter 8.

Throughout the book you will find short blurbs called Film Images. These are brief reviews of movies in which a character's vision impairment or blindness is a central part of the story. These blurbs are included in order to give you some idea of how visually impaired people are portrayed; you might want to rent these movies at your local video store and, as you watch, ask yourself if the characterization of the visually impaired person in the film seems accurate or realistic to you. You might find that these films will further enlighten you to the challenges and misconceptions of vision impairment.

Finally, at the end of the book, you will find a glossary of terms used in the text, a section of additional reading for you to use to continue your research, and a list of organizations and Web sites that can give you assistance and further information.

The topic of vision impairment is very large, with lots of information to be learned about both the facts and the emotions surrounding vision disorders and blindness. We hope this overview will serve as a good starting point for you to continue researching and learning everything you can about vision disorders.

Vision: An Overview

In this chapter you will get an overall sense of the most common vision disorders, as well as a basic knowledge of how vision works.

How Vision Works

In order to understand vision disorders, it helps to first understand how the eyes work.

Your ability to see depends on how good your eyes are at bending light. When light enters the eye, it is bent, or refracted so that it becomes focused on the back inside surface of the eye, or retina. Nearsightedness and farsightedness are both considered "refractive errors" because the light entering the eye is not being bent and focused in exactly the right way.

The ability to bend light depends upon the shape of the eye. You might think the eyeball is a perfectly round sphere, but it is really more of an oval. Nearsighted people's eyes are actually too long, so the light coming into them from distant objects is focused in front of, not on, the retina. The eyes of people with farsightedness are too short, causing light from close objects to focus behind the retina. Another common problem, called astigmatism, can happen by itself or with near- or farsightedness. Astigmatism is blurred vision that is caused by having a cornea with an uneven surface.

4

In addition to these refractive errors, many other things can go wrong and interfere with vision. These conditions include damage to any part of the eye, either from injury or disease. The result might be that a portion of one of the eye's structures wears away, or perhaps begins to grow incorrectly. Many vision problems are a result of aging.

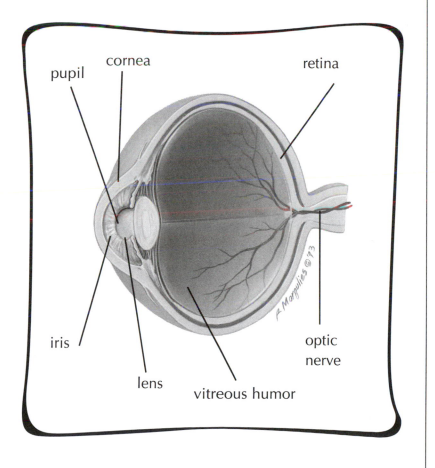

pupil

cornea

retina

iris

lens

vitreous humor

optic nerve

R. Margulies © '93

Luckily, refractive errors can now be corrected, and more research is in progress to discover new ways to save the sight of people who lose it to injury, disease, or aging.

Common Conditions

Nearsightedness, farsightedness, and astigmatism are the most common conditions teens have. These are usually inherited conditions—if you have impaired sight, chances are at least one of your parents has it too. These are also the most easily treatable conditions.

Nearsightedness

Nearsightedness, or myopia, makes it hard for a person to see things that are not close to him or her. Depending on how severe your nearsightedness is, you might have trouble reading street signs, seeing the blackboard in school, or even seeing things on the floor at your feet. You might prefer to sit closer to the television, but you probably have little trouble seeing the print in a book when you hold it in your hands.

Nearsightedness might worsen for a while and then level off for many years, only to begin to worsen again as the person ages.

Farsightedness

Farsightedness is less common among young people. It can be caused either by hyperopia, (when the eyeball is too short) or by presbyopia (a loss of elasticity in the eye, which causes most people over age fifty to need reading glasses). Farsightedness interferes with a person's ability to see things close-up. A farsighted person may need to hold a page at arm's length in order to read it.

6

Astigmatism

Astigmatism is blurred vision that is caused by having a cornea with an uneven surface. The cornea is the front layer of the eye, over the lens in the middle and the colored iris around the lens. In people with astigmatism, the cornea might be kind of wavy—flat in some spots and more steeply curved in others—causing the light coming through it to be transferred back to the retina in an uneven pattern. If you have astigmatism, it is likely that you can see vertical lines more clearly than horizontal ones or vice versa.

The 20/20 Standard

The 20/20 standard is the measure that is used to assess a person's eyesight. Vision that measures 20/20 is considered normal. If you have 20/20 vision, then you can see an object 20 feet away as well as other people with normal vision can see it. A higher second number, for example, 20/40, means you can see at 20 feet what a person with 20/20 vision can see at 40 feet.

In the United States, if a person's vision is no better than 20/200 in at least one eye, even with glasses or contacts, the person is considered legally blind. A person with 20/200 vision must be 20 feet from an object to see it, while a person with normal vision would be able to see the object from 200 feet away. For example, in a typical ice hockey rink, which is about 200 feet long, a referee with 20/20 vision should be able to stand at one end of the rink and see a puck on the ice all the way at the other end. If the referee has only 20/200 vision, however,

7

he would have to start skating toward the other end and get almost as close as the goal before he would be able to see the puck.

Kinds of Blindness

According to the National Association for Visually Handicapped, approximately 1,300,000 Americans are considered legally blind. People who have very limited vision or even legal blindness are sometimes referred to as having "low vision." Approximately 10 percent of those who are legally blind are completely sightless or can see just a slight amount of light.

Other forms of vision impairment include monocular blindness and color blindness. Monocular blindness is blindness in just one eye. Since the eyes work together to give you depth perception, with which you can tell how close or far away an object is, if you become blind in one eye you will have trouble with depth perception and will need time to adjust to this new way of seeing.

People who are color blind, or color vision deficient, usually have trouble telling the difference between reds and greens, although a rarer form affects how a person sees blues and yellows. The condition is hereditary, meaning it is passed on from parents to children, and affects males much more often than females.

What Causes Blindness

There are hundreds of conditions that can interfere with or steal your vision. These include conditions that are present at birth or that develop in early childhood as well as conditions that appear later in life. Some of these disorders are diseases specifically of the eyes, while others are not directly related to the eyes but have complications that affect vision.

Injuries and short-term illnesses can also cause permanent vision loss. It is estimated that of every 1,000 people in the United States, four to five of them are legally blind. The majority of blind people (around 65 percent) are over age sixty-five; a small minority of blind people (only about 5 percent) are under age twenty.

In the next three chapters, you will find information on many types of vision disorders and injuries. If you are familiar with the many disorders that can harm your eyesight then you will be less apt to, say, skip an eye doctor appointment or ignore signs of potential eye problems. Therefore, you will have a greater chance of keeping your vision at its absolute best.

Vision Problems in Babies and Children

It is relatively rare for a baby to be born blind, but many lose their sight soon after birth to infection or other preventable causes. If the mother has an infection, such as gonorrhea, she can pass it on to her baby at birth. For this reason, a baby's eyes are usually treated with silver nitrate or an antibiotic solution just after birth. If the mother has rubella early in her pregnancy, it can affect her baby's vision. Malnutrition and parasitic infections can also endanger a baby's eyesight, as well as its life in general. Some conditions that can affect the sight of a newborn baby or young child are described in the sections that follow.

Retinopathy of Prematurity

This condition is present at birth in premature babies and causes loss of vision in approximately 2,600 infants in the United States each year, according to the National Alliance for Eye and Vision Research. It is caused by changes in the blood vessels of the retina that occur soon after birth

Strabismus

Strabismus occurs when the eyes are out of alignment with each other. They may appear "crossed" or one eye may seem to be looking to the side while the other is looking forward. In a person with strabismus, the eyes are not working in tandem to produce a single image. Instead, each eye is sending the brain its own version of what the person is looking at. This often causes blurred or double vision and is very confusing for the brain, which eventually begins to ignore the image that one of the eyes is sending it. The eye that is ignored will eventually become "lazy," or unused, and after a while of being unused, the eye will actually become blind. The scientific term for "lazy eye" is amblyopia. Amblyopia can also occur when one eye is much weaker than the other, even if the eyes are not out of alignment.

Strabismus can be very hard to detect; it might not be as obvious as crossed eyes. Sometimes the misalignment is so slight that you can't detect it simply by looking at the person. Still, even a slight misalignment can cause potentially permanent problems such as amblyopia, the leading cause of single-eye blindness.

In addition to losing the sight in one eye, a person with single-eye blindness also loses the ability to see things in three dimensions. This ability is called depth perception. Without it, a person may experience difficulty judging the height of a step or how far to reach for an object and may find it very difficult to catch or hit a ball.

Strabismus can be corrected if it is detected in time; for this reason, it is very important for children to have regular eye examinations, starting no later than six months after birth. From birth to age three or four months, it is normal for a baby's eyes to wander independently. By six months, however, according to Prevent Blindness America, an infant's eyes should be moving together and he or she should be able to focus on both near and far objects. If a condition like amblyopia is not detected until the child is about to start school, it may already be too late to correct it. Treatment for strabismus and amblyopia can include glasses, an eye patch, medicated eyedrops, eye exercises, or surgery. It is crucial that treatment begin as soon as possible for children who are found to have these conditions very early in life.

Color Blindness

Color blindness, or color vision deficiency, is most often caused by a genetic condition. It limits a person's ability to see color, but almost never removes it entirely.

The ability to see colors comes from cells within the retina called cone cells. Cone cells and their partners, rod cells, work together to convert the light that comes into the eye and turn it into electrical impulses that travel back into the brain and are interpreted as visual images. The rod cells read only light, while the cone cells read both light and color. Rod cells outnumber cone cells by twenty to one, and cone cells need much more light than rod cells in order to function. This is why it is harder to tell differences among colors in dim light.

There are three different types of cone cells. Each type "sees" one of the colors red, green, or blue. Some people have defective cone cells. This condition, commonly known as color blindness, occurs in about 8 percent of males but less than 1 percent of females. Color blindness, or more accurately, color vision deficiency, is almost never a significant handicap, which is fortunate because there is no cure for it. People who have it usually have trouble with reds and greens; much less common is a form of color vision deficiency affecting a person's ability to see yellows and blues. It is extremely rare for a person to be unable to see any colors.

While most cases of color vision deficiency are hereditary, some people develop it as they age and the eyes'
lenses begin to darken. Some medications and eye diseases can also interfere with color vision.

A typical eye exam includes testing for color vision deficiency. The test might involve reading numbers created in
a red-and-green design; a color-vision-deficient person
will see different numbers than a person with correct
color vision will see.

Sometimes people can have just a slight problem with
one color, a problem so slight that it won't even register
on the color-vision test, and they might never even know
they have it.

Albinism

Albinism is a genetic disorder in which the person's body
does not produce melanin, the substance that gives color to
the skin, hair, and eyes. The lack of melanin in the eyes
causes vision to develop improperly by affecting the optic
nerve and the fovea, an area of the retina. People with
albinism rarely have normal vision, but in most cases their
vision can be at least somewhat improved with glasses or
contacts. In addition to extreme near- or farsightedness,
albinism often causes strabismus or a condition called nystagmus, in which the eyes move involuntarily back and forth.

One myth about albinism that is not true is that all
people who have the condition have red or pink eyes. In
fact, people with albinism often have colored eyes,
although they might be pale, and you might be able to see
an occasional flash of red through their pupils, similar to

what "red eye" in a photograph looks like. While many people with the condition lack pigment in their hair and skin, others show its effects only in their eyes, so you can't always tell just by looking at someone that he or she has albinism.

There are a number of other relatively rare hereditary conditions that can cause low vision or blindness in children. These include:

- Choroideremia, a rare condition that almost always affects males

- Leber congenital amaurosis (LCA), which generally causes severe loss of vision at birth

- Juvenile retinoschisis, a condition affecting mostly males that begins at birth but may not show symptoms until after age ten

- Bardet-Biedl syndrome, in which the sufferer is almost always born with extra fingers and toes and experiences other difficulties including obesity and problems with the kidneys

- Usher syndrome, which also causes deafness and is the leading cause when a child is both deaf and blind

All of these conditions cause damage to the retina and are genetically inherited. They are not curable, although genetic research has revealed the affected genes in some of these conditions. This research may someday lead to treatment for these diseases or even ways to prevent them.

Progressive Conditions and Accidents

As people age, their eyesight tends to become weaker. You may have had perfect vision as a child, but as you entered the teen years perhaps you needed glasses for the first time. Likewise, even people who have been lucky enough to have 20/20 vision all of their lives may find they need reading glasses when they reach their forties or fifties. This is very common and normal.

Besides the natural growing and aging process and the need for vision correction that can go with it, there are many conditions that can gradually steal a person's sight. These conditions are called "progressive" because they will progress, or continue, becoming worse over time. Some of these diseases can be treated so that they are stopped from progressing.

Retinitis Pigmentosa

This condition, actually a group of diseases, is hereditary, and it causes the retina to break down. It can begin in childhood. The cause or causes of retinitis pigmentosa (RP) are not known, but for some reason the rod cells of the retina begin to deteriorate. The first sign of RP is poor night vision, followed by the loss of peripheral vision. Eventually, this condition results in tunnel vision, in which the person can see only through a small area of the eye and only straight ahead. In more severe cases of RP, the cone cells may be affected as well.

A person with a healthy field of vision can see 180 degrees, or the entire half-spherical area in front of them, up and down, and to each side. Tunnel vision takes away most of the peripheral vision, reducing the size of the visual field. In the United States, a person is considered legally blind if his or her field of vision becomes narrower than twenty degrees, or one-ninth the width of a normal field of vision; this is often a consequence of retinitis pigmentosa.

Prevent Blindness America reports that retinitis pigmentosa and related conditions affect approximately 400,000 Americans. RP is the leading cause of blindness from an inherited condition, and there is currently no known treatment. However, the National Alliance for Eye and Vision Research reports that progress has been made in identifying the genes responsible for this disease, which could eventually lead to treatment.

Diabetic Retinopathy

This disease can occur in people who have diabetes and is the leading cause of blindness in people under age sixty. Diabetics are twenty-five times more likely to lose their sight than are nondiabetics. All diabetics should have frequent eye exams so that diabetic retinopathy can be caught in its early stages, when it is treatable. Diabetic retinopathy occurs when small blood vessels in the retina begin to leak blood, causing permanent blurred vision. New blood vessels begin to grow on the retina, but they are weak and they leak blood into the eyeball, again causing blurred vision.

In many cases, these leaking blood vessels can be repaired with laser surgery, but any vision that has been lost will not come back. The chances of developing diabetic retinopathy are greater the longer a person has the disease, so it is very important that diabetics do their best to manage their disease through diet, exercise, medication, and close contact with their doctors.

Glaucoma

Glaucoma is caused by too much pressure inside the eyeball. A normal eye is filled with fluid that the body replaces on a regular basis: New fluid is produced and added to the eye, while old fluid drains from the eye. If new fluid comes in faster than the old fluid can drain out, or if the drainage path is blocked, glaucoma is the result. As pressure builds in the eye, blood flow is cut off to the retina and the optic nerve, damaging vision or even causing blindness.

Glaucoma may be either acute or chronic. Acute glaucoma is an emergency: It means that the drainage path from one or both eyes has suddenly become completely blocked. This is extremely painful and requires immediate medical attention to save the sight in the affected eye. Chronic glaucoma usually builds up over several years, and you might not know you have it. Glaucoma usually affects adults over forty, but it can sometimes occur in babies and children or as a result of injuries. Prevent Blindness America estimates that one in thirty people over age forty has glaucoma, and half of those people don't know they have it.

Glaucoma is another condition that can be treated if it is caught early. Treatment might include laser surgery or medication to lower pressure within the eye and keep it at a safe level. As with diabetic retinopathy, any sight that is lost will not come back, but treatment can prevent more damage. The risk of blindness from glaucoma is another reason why it is so important for everyone to have regular eye exams. Over two million Americans have glaucoma, and approximately 120,000 are blind as a result of it. Glaucoma is the leading cause of blindness among African Americans, who are four to five times more likely than Caucasians to develop the condition. People who are very nearsighted or who have diabetes are also at higher risk for glaucoma.

When you have an eye exam, you might be given a glaucoma test in which a machine sends a puff of air into your eye. This test can be scary because the puff of air might startle you, and it can be hard to keep your eye open when you know the puff is coming, but it is not painful and nothing actually touches your eye. After a few exams, you will get used to this test, and knowing how important it is should make it easier to tolerate.

Cataracts

A cataract is a cloudy area in the lens of the eye. It can happen in one or both eyes. Cataracts are usually caused by aging. As a person gets older, the lenses of the eyes start to wear out. The National Alliance for Eye and Vision Research estimates that about 29 percent of all people between the ages of sixty-five and seventy-four have cataracts. Young people can also get cataracts, though, usually from an injury, eye infection, or disease. Some researchers suspect a link to cigarette smoking as well. Animals can get cataracts, too; if you have an older dog, you might be able to see signs of cataracts in his or her eyes.

Looking through a cataract is described as being like seeing the world through a gray fog or mist. Some people have cataracts but are still able to see fairly well. Over time, though, cataracts tend to get worse. When the cataracts start to interfere with your vision enough to reduce your quality of life, surgery is usually recommended. The surgeon removes the cloudy lens and replaces it with something similar to a permanent contact lens. "My grandma had her cataracts taken out," one boy reported, "and now she can see further down our street than I can!" Cataract surgery has become very common and is almost always successful. Cataracts used to cause thousands of cases of blindness every year, but now that the surgery to correct them has become more reliable and less feared, cataracts do not have to lead to permanent loss of sight.

Hypertensive Retinal Bleeding

High blood pressure, or hypertension, can cause bleeding in the retina, which can lead to scarring and damaged vision. People with high blood pressure might have changes in the retina and still have normal vision, but these changes are still important because they alert the ophthalmologist to possible problems in other parts of the body that are vulnerable to damage from hypertension. The kidneys and heart are especially susceptible to damage from high blood pressure.

Papilledema

Papilledema is the atrophy or death of the optic nerve. It is usually caused by increased pressure inside the skull, which can result from high blood pressure or from a growth in the brain. As the optic nerve is squeezed, vision slowly becomes poor. Vision can be restored if this condition is treated in time.

Macular Degeneration

There is an area in the center of the retina that contains a great number of rod and cone cells. This area, called the macula, allows you to see fine details such as small print or a tiny splinter in your finger. As you age, the macula can break down, causing you to lose the sight in the center of your field of vision. Macular degeneration does not affect peripheral vision, so people who have it are still able to see, but they cannot make out fine details and images are blurry. Reading is difficult and driving is no longer possible.

Approximately 1.7 million people suffer from decreased vision as a result of macular degeneration, and 100,000 are blind. In fact, age-related macular degeneration (AMD) is the most common cause of severe visual impairment in older Americans. However, many people are able to use their outer field of vision to see well enough to care for themselves. Some people with the disease find that they are still able to read through the use of powerful magnifiers.

Macular degeneration is painless and generally develops slowly. The exact causes are not known, but it is believed to be at least partially hereditary and some researchers suspect a link with arteriosclerosis, cigarette smoking, or injuries to the eye. In some cases, it is partially treatable, and promising research may make it possible to transplant healthy cells into the retina to restore sight.

In addition to the age-related form of macular degeneration, there are some conditions that cause macular degeneration in children and young adults. These include Stargardt disease and Best disease, both of which are genetically inherited conditions. Best disease begins as a bright yellow cyst, or fluid-filled sac, behind the macula. If you have this condition, you might still have good or fairly good vision, even with the cyst. Also, the disease does not always affect both eyes equally, so you might find that you have one "good eye" that gives you better vision than the other. Eventually, the cyst is likely to break, and at that point your vision will begin to deteriorate further. People with Best disease are often farsighted as well, a condition that can be corrected with glasses. The disease itself, however, has no treatment. The Foundation Fighting Blindness notes that in people who have Best disease, "central vision tends to deteriorate to about 20/100 late in life. However . . . many individuals retain useful central vision in one eye with a visual acuity of about 20/40 in the lesser affected eye."

Stargardt disease is similar to Best disease in that it involves the presence of yellowish spots on the macula. In Stargardt disease, however, there are a number of small, individual spots instead of one large cyst. Stargardt disease, the most common form of inherited juvenile macular degeneration, usually does more damage to your vision. The Foundation Fighting Blindness states that "almost all individuals with Stargardt disease are expected to have visual acuities in the range of 20/200 to 20/400," which would be considered legally blind. Like Best disease, Stargardt disease currently has no treatment, but promising research is underway. The gene responsible for Stargardt disease was isolated in 1997; researchers can now study what happens when the gene mutates, information that could lead to a treatment for the condition.

Cancer

Cancer can steal vision by affecting the eyes themselves or the brain. One form of cancer that affects the eyes is called retinoblastoma. It is often curable by removal of the tumor that grows in the eye, and vision can often be saved in at least one eye. Melanoma, a cancer that usually grows on the skin and is believed to be related to overexposure to the sun, can also occur in the eyes. This form of cancer may also be treatable, depending on where in the eye it occurs and how advanced it is when it is discovered. There are many forms of brain cancer that can also affect vision.

Sudden Vision Impairment

Any sudden loss of vision is serious and should be treated as an emergency. Below are just a few of the problems that can cause sudden vision impairment.

Detached Retina
Sudden loss of sight in a portion or all of your field of vision, in one or both eyes, can be a sign of a detached retina. The retina is a very thin layer of cells that lines the back of the inside of your eye. It can peel away from its

backing, causing you to see a shower of sparks or what seems like a curtain being pulled across part or all of your field of vision. Retinal detachment is often the result of a head injury, but it can happen as the result of a variety of eye diseases or without any obvious cause. If it is caught in time and you receive immediate surgery by an ophthalmologist, the retina can usually be reattached successfully. If the retina is not reattached, or if too much time passes and the cells in the retina have already died, you will have permanent loss of sight. Never ignore signs such as flashing lights or blank areas in your field of vision.

Impact Injuries

Anything that falls or flies into your eyes or hits you in the head or face could harm your vision. Hitting your head as a result of a fall, car accident, or other mishap could cost you your sight. In fact, car accidents are the leading cause of eye injuries in young children, according to Prevent Blindness America. That organization also estimates that 90 percent of all eye injuries in children could be prevented or made less severe if people knew more about common eye dangers.

Some common warnings you've probably heard from parents and teachers are to avoid throwing sharp objects like pencils, make sure no one is in your way when you swing a bat or golf club, and never run while carrying scissors.

You should see a doctor any time you take a hard hit to the head, especially if you black out or feel dizzy or confused afterward, if there is any bleeding, or if you have any visual disturbances such as double vision, blurred vision, flashing lights, floating spots, or blank or dark areas in your field of vision. You might have a concussion or a skull fracture, both of which need to be treated and monitored for complications. The same is true of any injury to your eyes: If something pokes you in the eye, you should see a doctor to check for scratches on your cornea. If an object is embedded in your eye, do not pull it out! Leave the object there and find someone to help you carefully cover both of your eyes (even if only one is hurt) to prevent them from moving. If the object is sticking out too far to bandage over it, have your helper find something that will fit over it, such as a small paper cup, and tape that covering in place. Then get to an emergency room immediately.

Burns

You might have heard that you can damage your eyes by looking directly into the sun, especially during an eclipse. This is true. Do not look directly at an eclipse, even for a second. You might think you can peek at it, and when you find that it doesn't hurt right away, you might be tempted to look longer. Unfortunately, even if it doesn't hurt right away, you might still be damaging your retinas, and it will eventually hurt very badly. Besides the pain, these burns can cause permanent vision loss. Looking at the sun through a telescope will cause even more severe damage.

Chemical burns are also dangerous to your sight. If you ever get any type of chemical in your eyes, get help immediately to prevent permanent damage. Some products have instructions on the label telling you what to do if it gets into your eyes. Follow these instructions if you can, but get to a doctor as soon as possible for further treatment.

Glasses, Contacts, and Surgery

It is estimated that about half the population needs some form of vision correction. This may be due to myopia, hyperopia, presbyopia, astigmatism, some combination of any of these conditions, or even some other condition altogether. Most people with one of these conditions can have their vision corrected fairly easily by wearing glasses or contact lenses. Recently, surgeries that correct poor vision have become very popular, although they are rarely covered by insurance.

Corrective Lenses

Most cases of near- and farsightedness and astigmatism can be corrected, or at least improved, with glasses or contact lenses. Nearsightedness, or myopia, is generally more of a problem in daily life than farsightedness because it makes it difficult to see the blackboard in school and can cause problems with coordination in sports. Nearsightedness is also problematic for teens and adults because it impairs a person's ability to drive. Each state has its own guidelines, but in general, vision must be corrected to very close to normal for a person to get a driver's license. For people with severe vision problems, their corrective lenses become the key to a full life.

Glasses or contacts?

The choice of whether to have glasses or contacts is often a trade-off between fashion and expense. Many people, especially kids, don't like to wear glasses because they don't like the way they look. But glasses are generally less expensive than contacts, and so the choice might depend on what the person, or his or her parents, can afford. Glasses can also be a very cool fashion accessory! However, contacts make more sense for people who are very active or who need excellent peripheral, or side, vision (for example, soccer players).

Besides their most common use, correcting nearsightedness, glasses can also be adapted for other needs. Special glasses can be used as a treatment for amblyopia. Glasses can be fitted with lenses that resemble binoculars for people with very poor vision. Sunglasses are often prescribed for people whose eyes are especially sensitive to light, such as those with albinism or people who have recently had cataract surgery or another form of eye surgery. Sunglasses are, of course, one of the most recognizable symbols of coolness, and so most people don't mind wearing them. You can have sunglasses made with your vision correction prescription in the lenses, so you can see where you're going, protect your eyes, and still look cool.

Going to the Ophthalmologist

An ophthalmologist (pronounced OP-tha-MA-luh-jist) is a doctor who specializes in diagnosing and treating vision problems. When you visit the ophthalmologist, there are a few things to keep in mind:

- Before you go, pay attention to the specific kinds of problems you are encountering. Write them down and bring these notes to the appointment so you don't forget to tell everything to the doctor.

- Likewise, write down any questions you have. You may want more information about glasses, contacts, or surgery. Don't be afraid to ask! If the doctor's response is unclear to you, ask for clarification.

- Have someone, preferably a parent, accompany you to an eye exam. Eyedrops are put in your eyes to dilate the pupils (this makes it easier for the doctor to see inside your eye). Pupils usually contract to keep out the glare of bright light, so everything will appear really bright to you for a few hours afterward, and you won't be able to drive yourself home. And bring sunglasses!

- After receiving your glasses or contacts, be very sensitive to how well they are working. If the prescription doesn't feel quite right, or if your eyesight changes again, call the doctor right away—don't wait!

Specially tinted glasses can in some cases help people with color vision deficiency to distinguish the colors that they are unable to see.

Refractive Surgery

As an alternative to glasses and contact lenses, surgery is sometimes performed to correct the refractive errors of near- and farsightedness. All of these procedures are usually performed with local anesthetic, meaning that you stay awake during them, and they do not require a hospital stay. Refractive surgery can make a significant difference in a person's quality of life, but it is not usually covered by insurance.

The first form of surgery developed to correct myopia was radial keratotomy (RK), which involves the cutting of the cornea in a pattern like the spokes of a wheel to change its shape. These cuts allow the cornea to flatten out, which creates improved focusing ability. The cuts must be made very precisely in order to achieve just the right amount of flattening of the cornea. The American Society of Cataract and Refractive Surgery notes that in a study sponsored by the National Eye Institute that examined the success rate of RK over the previous ten years, seven out of ten patients still did not need corrective lenses ten years after having the surgery.

Other surgical techniques have been developed since RK. These include astigmatic keratotomy (AK), used to treat astigmatism. It is performed in the same manner as RK, but the incisions are made in a different pattern. RK and AK can be performed at the same time.

Two forms of laser surgery to correct refractive errors have also been developed. Photorefractive keratectomy (PRK) and laser in-situ keratomileusis (LASIK) both use lasers to remove a microscopic portion of the cornea and improve its focusing ability. In PRK, the laser removes a layer from the surface of the cornea, while in LASIK, the surgeon cuts and lays back a thin flap of the cornea, then uses the laser to remove a small layer from the underlying portion of the cornea, and finally replaces the corneal flap, which goes back into place without any stitches.

Another form of surgery that does not involve reshaping or removing tissue from the cornea is called Intacs. This procedure involves the implantation of tiny, specially shaped bits of plastic that change the shape of the front surface of the eye, thereby correcting refractive errors. This new procedure is still in the testing stages, but early data indicates that 98 percent of patients undergoing the procedure are able to see at a level of 20/40 or better one year after surgery.

All of these surgical techniques carry risks and can result in complications. While the rates of negative results are low, it is important to consider them when making a decision as to whether or not to have surgery. Possible complications include seeing a glare or halos around objects, fluctuations in your vision, double vision, light sensitivity, haze or shadow images, increased pressure within the eye, overcorrection or undercorrection, or even a worsening of vision. As with all surgeries, there is also a risk of infection or of a reaction to the anesthesia.

Surgery is not a good idea for children because their eyes will continue to change, sometimes radically, as they grow from teenagers to young adults. Your eyesight and therefore

Film Images: *At First Sight*

An architect (Mira Sorvino) falls in love with a blind massage therapist (Val Kilmer). He seems well adjusted to a sightless life, but she convinces him to undergo an experimental surgery that may give him limited vision. The surgery is a success, but it impacts the relationship in unexpected ways. Based on a true story. PG-13; 1999.

your prescription for corrective lenses might change every six months; getting new glasses twice a year may be expensive, but still possible, while having surgery every six months is neither practical nor desirable. If you believe you would like to have surgery to correct near- or farsightedness, do some research now and learn everything you can about the different procedures. Then keep up with new developments in the field so that you will be well informed about your options when you are old enough to decide whether to have the surgery. Procedures that are currently in development and may be available to you in the future include laser thermal keratoplasty (LTK), a procedure intended to correct farsightedness; radio frequency keratoplasty (RTK), a procedure similar to LTK that uses radio waves instead of a laser; and phakic intraocular lenses, which are permanently implanted lenses similar to those used in cataract surgery but that do not require the removal of the original lens.

Other Treatments for Vision Problems

While glasses and contacts are probably the most common form of vision correction, there are many other ways to help a person with a vision problem. Some of these techniques are discussed in this chapter.

Patches

When an eye problem is the result of incorrect muscle movement or of one eye being much stronger than the other, a patch can be used to help restore balance and correct functioning. Patching the stronger eye and making the weaker eye do all of the work some of the time can force the weaker eye to become stronger. This technique can also keep the brain from rejecting signals from the weaker eye, since those signals will be the only ones it receives when the stronger eye is taking a break. Keeping signals from both eyes going into the brain, even if it's from one eye at a time, can help prevent blindness in the weaker eye. Eventually the weaker eye will become strong enough to work together with the stronger eye, and the patch will no longer be needed.

Medications

Medications, often in eyedrop form, can be used to treat some conditions, including strabismus, amblyopia, and glaucoma. These conditions also have surgical procedures that can be used if the medication does not work, but it is always better to exhaust all the possibilities of correcting the problem with medication before resorting to surgery.

Medications to control conditions that can affect vision, such as diabetes and high blood pressure, are also very important. Even if you experience no symptoms if you skip your medication or fail to monitor your blood sugar levels, you could be damaging your sight. These conditions must be managed very precisely and carefully if you want to avoid vision impairment. If some vision has already been lost, careful attention to your treatment regimen can help to prevent further deterioration of your remaining sight.

Exercises and Biofeedback

In some cases, eye exercises and biofeedback have been used to treat conditions such as strabismus and amblyopia. Both of these treatments retrain the muscles of the eye to work properly. Biofeedback is a method of making the patient aware of functions of the body that we don't normally pay attention to, such as heartbeat. By learning to recognize through biofeedback when the eye muscles are or are not doing what they're supposed to do, you can begin to control them.

Diet

If you have diabetes, controlling your diet is very important. Even if you take insulin, you still must make sure that you are eating the things you should and avoiding the things you shouldn't have. You may feel fine and think that you don't need to watch your sugar intake or measure your blood sugar levels, but fluctuations that you can't feel can do damage without you knowing it. In order to avoid permanent damage to your vision, you must manage your condition more precisely than simply relying on how you feel. Another condition that can be helped or harmed by your diet is high blood pressure, or hypertension, which can increase your risk of developing glaucoma. If you have been told by your doctor to follow a special diet to help keep your hypertension under control, do it—it's better to go without some foods you like or eat them less often than it is to lose your sight.

Surgery

Just as surgical solutions have been developed for nearsightedness, farsightedness, and astigmatism, surgery can also be used to correct eye muscle abnormalities such as strabismus, to reduce pressure inside the eye caused by glaucoma, to repair a torn or detached retina, to remove cataracts, and to replace damaged corneas. Surgery is also used to remove tumors of the eye and brain that can affect vision.

Cataract Surgery

A cataract is a cloudy area of the lens of the eye. Many senior citizens have cataracts, which are a natural side effect of aging, but they can also occur in younger people as a result of an injury or illness such as diabetes or high blood pressure. Sometimes cataracts are congenital and babies are born with them.

The only treatment for cataracts is surgery; there are no drugs or eyedrops that will improve or cure cataracts. In cataract surgery, which is usually performed on an outpatient basis and with local anesthesia, the damaged lens is replaced with an artificial lens, much like a contact lens that fits over the eye, except in this case the lens is implanted permanently inside the eye where the original lens used to be. This intraocular lens, or IOL, has eliminated the need for cataract patients to wear thick glasses after surgery. The American Society of Cataract and Refractive Surgery reports that 95 percent of patients undergoing cataract surgery experience a significant improvement in their vision and have no complications.

Eye Muscle Surgery

Imbalances in the strength of the eye muscles can cause conditions such as strabismus and nystagmus. If other techniques such as patching and drops do not work, surgery can be performed to weaken or strengthen the affected muscles and bring the eyes back into alignment. In the case of strabismus, if surgery is performed before permanent vision loss has occurred, it can prevent damage to a child's vision. However, the surgery can also be performed on adults as a cosmetic correction, to improve the appearance of the eyes and make them "match," even if it is too late to save the vision in the affected eye.

Glaucoma Surgery

Glaucoma, which results from excessive pressure within the eye, can often be treated with medication. Occasionally, however, the pressure within the eye becomes too severe for medication to correct, or an acute blockage of the draining of fluid from the eye occurs. These situations require surgery to bring the fluid level inside the eye back into balance.

Glaucoma is caused either by too much fluid going into the eye or by fluid not draining out quickly enough. Surgery can change either of these conditions. In order to decrease the rate at which fluid enters the eye, the surgeon can use a form of cryosurgery or a laser to destroy some of the ciliary processes, the structures within the eye that produce the fluid. Destroying them, either with the cold of cryosurgery or the heat of laser surgery, renders them unable to produce fluid and allows the current rate of natural drainage to reduce the pressure within the eye to acceptable levels.

The second approach, increasing the rate at which fluid drains from the eye, can be accomplished with traditional surgical methods or with a laser. The procedure involves creating a hole in the trabecular meshwork, the structure through which fluid drains from the eye. This new opening in the trabecular meshwork, which can be made by cutting an incision or burning a hole with the laser, gives the fluid another exit and therefore allows it to drain more quickly.

Another form of surgery redirects the flow of fluid from the eye when it is obstructed as a result of a less common form of glaucoma known as angle closure glaucoma. In this procedure, a hole is made in the iris to allow the fluid a more direct route to the trabecular meshwork.

Corneal Transplants

People whose visual impairments are due to injury or disease of the cornea can often have their sight restored with a corneal transplant. Corneas are one of the organs and tissues that can be transplanted from one person to another, and many people sign organ-donor cards allowing their corneas to be used in the event of their death. Corneas must be preserved immediately and the transplant must take place within two to three days in order to be successful. The first eye bank was established in 1945 in New York City to collect and preserve donated corneas; since then most other major cities have followed suit, and now every major medical center in the United States has an eye bank.

Surgery for Retinal Detachment

A detached retina is an emergency that threatens a person's vision. It can be caused by an injury, but it can also happen as a complication of nearsightedness or diseases such as diabetes. If it is not brought on by an injury or blow to the eye, retinal detachment usually begins with a hole in the retina. The fluid inside the eye leaks through this hole, getting between the retina and the wall of the eye and allowing the retina to peel away like wallpaper.

Retinal detachment is often a result of aging. As people grow older, the amount of vitreous fluid in their eyes can become gradually reduced, lowering the pressure that keeps the retina pressed firmly against the inside of the eye and allowing the retina to slump away from the eye. Regular eye exams can detect a developing problem before it leads to retinal detachment.

There are a number of different surgical techniques that can be used to repair holes in the retina and retinal detachments. Some involve the use of lasers to create small bits of scar tissue that seal the retina back onto the inside of the eye. Other techniques require an incision and possibly the removal of the vitreous fluid inside the eye, allowing the surgeon to use air or gas to fill the eye and push the retina back into position. The body eventually replaces the vitreous fluid on its own.

Cancer Treatment

Cancers of the eye and brain often are treated with a combination of surgery to remove the tumor and radiation or chemotherapy to destroy any remaining cancer cells and prevent the problem from recurring. These cancers, like all forms of cancer, are very serious, and the treatment can be painful. If you have a tumor in your eye or a brain tumor that is affecting your vision, your doctors will do everything they can to save the sight in at least one of your eyes, but their top priority will be saving your life. It might be hard for you to think about the possibility of going through this long and painful treatment only to end up with low or no vision, but it would be better for you to survive the disease and lose your sight than to lose your life because you refused the treatment.

A diagnosis of cancer is one of the most challenging things a person can have to deal with. If you have cancer, please make sure that you are using every resource available to you for information, emotional support, and medical advice. Your parents and friends can help you to gather information about your condition and they can help you to cope with the treatment process and the prognosis, or predicted results, for your particular illness. The Where to Go for Help section at the end of this book also contains information on many organizations that can give you and your family more assistance.

Future Goals

There is much research currently in progress to find treatments and preventive measures for vision disorders. Many people and organizations are devoted to the goal of finding new ways to help people who have lost some or all of their sight, and also to preventing vision loss from disease or accidents.

Retinal Chip

A possible future treatment for blindness, the retinal chip, became news in early 1999. This device might one day be used to restore some vision to people whose optic nerves are still healthy despite a breakdown of retinal functioning. This tiny computer chip would be implanted on the surface of the retina and would be used in conjunction with a pair of special glasses containing a camera to transmit visual information to the brain. While this technology is not expected to give people full, clear vision, it is hoped that it will provide a level of sight that is good enough to allow a person greater mobility and independence.

Treatment of Diabetic Complications

Researchers have succeeded in cloning aldose reductase (AR), an enzyme implicated in diabetic vision problems.

This breakthrough in turn led to the development of AR inhibitors, which are expected to eventually allow for the prevention of many of the visual complications of diabetes.

Gene Therapy

Research into the causes of genetically based vision disorders has isolated the genes responsible for retinoblastoma (a form of cancer) and retinitis pigmentosa and has produced important clues to the genetic basis of juvenile onset glaucoma. It is hoped that this research will lead to ways to prevent or treat these and other conditions.

Cell Transplants

The National Alliance for Eye and Vision Research reports that "the scientific basis has been established for transplanting healthy cells into the retina to restore sight." Further refinement of this technique could lead to a treatment for macular degeneration and retinitis pigmentosa.

Emotional Issues If You Have a Severe Vision Disorder

In this chapter we will examine some of the feelings you are likely to have when you are confronted with a vision disorder, along with some suggestions for dealing with your feelings and the reactions of your friends, family, fellow students or coworkers, and the strangers you will encounter.

This chapter also includes encouraging words from organizations that work to help people with vision disorders and to educate sighted people about the facts and myths of low vision and blindness.

If You Have a Severe Vision Disorder

If you were born sighted and have recently been diagnosed with a condition that is likely to damage or destroy your vision, it is normal for you to feel all kinds of different, sometimes even conflicting or contradictory, feelings. A common initial reaction to such a diagnosis is fear—fear of being blind, fear of losing the life that you know, fear of being abandoned by the people you care about, fear of not being able to accomplish the goals you have for yourself. It is natural and normal to feel this way. How could you be expected not to be afraid of such a huge change? At this point you have no idea how you

Blindness is something that just about everyone fears. In fact, only cancer and AIDS rank higher on the list of dreaded conditions for most people. This is especially significant when you consider that AIDS and cancer are life threatening, while loss of vision by itself is not.

Much of this fear stems from a lack of knowledge about what it is really like to be blind. According to the Foundation Fighting Blindness, "Before their own loss of sight, few people personally know the many blind individuals with active, useful lives, making negative images of blindness hard to refute." If you have never been around a blind person or seen how someone with a visual impairment manages day-to-day life, it would be natural for you to think that low vision or blindness would be very limiting and could ruin your life. However, this is simply not true. "When you are newly blind, in the beginning, it can feel frustrating or scary," says the National Federation of the Blind. "This is because you have not learned how to do things for yourself as a blind person. But once you learn the skills that blind people use, you no longer feel that way."

will manage to do everything you do now, and you have no idea how people will react to you. Along with being frightened, you are likely to feel vulnerable, weak, endangered, isolated, and alone.

Working Through Emotions

Shortly after feeling fear, you might begin to feel angry. In fact, you might become enraged at the unfairness of your loss of sight. This all-consuming anger can cause you to demand answers—answers that no one has—to questions like "Why me?" "Why is there no cure for this?" "Why does this have to happen?" "What did I do to deserve this?" or even "How am I going to live if I can't see?" Like fear, anger and even rage are normal reactions to the news that you might lose your sight. No one should expect you to take it calmly, like some stoic, long-suffering martyr. In fact, it would be unhealthy for you to try to hide or bottle up your feelings.

From feeling anger you might shift into denial, reasoning that if you refuse to accept this, it won't happen. This is the point at which you will tell everyone, "I don't need any help!" or you refuse to make accommodations for your loss of vision because you insist it will be just a temporary condition. You will try to do all of the same things you did before, and you might have some accidents that will serve only to bring back the anger that is still there under the surface.

As a result you might sink into depression. An attitude of "I give up" or "I don't care" is common at this stage. You might refuse to take any action to learn about your condition or to develop new skills and coping methods; you might not even feel like bathing or eating or even getting out of bed. Your thoughts might sound something like this: "What's the use? Why get up when I'm just going to sit around all day doing nothing anyway? Might as well just sleep." Experts say it can take an average of six months to work through your initial reaction and reach a point where you are ready to work toward solutions to dealing with your vision impairment.

These feelings will be hard enough to handle, but on top of your reaction to your condition, you will have to deal with the reactions of your family members, friends, and classmates, all of whom will have their own crisis reaction to your news and all of whom will also react to *your* reaction. Unfortunately, without meaning to, these people can make it even harder for you. If you are fortunate, though, there will be at least one person who will be able to help you in the ways you need to be helped, even if you don't yet know what those ways are.

Other People's Feelings

When you learn that you might lose your sight, your focus and the focus of everyone in your life should be on helping you to deal with the news. However, it is important for you to realize that everyone in your life will also be experiencing their own strong feelings in reaction to what's happening to you. Just as you are fearful or angry or depressed, the people who care about you might feel afraid for you or angry or sad that this is happening to you. At times it might seem that the people around you are more upset for themselves because of what's happening to you than they are actually upset for you.

It is a fact of our psychological makeup that each person tends to experience the world primarily as it affects him or her, and only secondarily as it affects others. Most people make a conscious effort to overcome this, but in emotionally-charged situations, many people think about

43

their own feelings first and therefore might at times neglect yours. Just when you most need their support, others might be thinking about how hard it is for them to handle what's happening.

For example, some parents react so dramatically when their children are injured or ill that the children learn to downplay their symptoms just so their parents won't freak out. When the person in crisis is you, but you're having to worry about not upsetting the people who are supposed to be supporting you, it makes it that much harder for you to cope.

Having some understanding of what the people around you are likely to be experiencing might help you to keep your perspective if your raw emotions collide with theirs and arguments or hurt feelings begin to erupt. When you're ready, it can help to invite the others to talk about how what's happening to you is making them feel. Once you give people permission to talk about what might seem to them to be selfish feelings, they will probably feel very relieved to be able to share those feelings with you.

You might find that, for example, the reason your best friend hasn't come to visit you is because he is afraid to think about how he would feel if he were you. He probably wants very much to help you, but his own fear is holding him back. Or you might discover that your mother's maddening habit of hovering over you and watching you like a hawk is rooted in a sense of guilt that she could have somehow prevented this from happening to you if she had only been "a better mother." Sometimes speaking these types of feelings out loud takes away some of their power and allows you to cope with them. And once you and everyone around you have sorted through your initial reactions to the situation, you can all get down to the business of learning to adapt to your vision disorder.

Accepting Reality

It can take a long time to accept the truth of what is happening to you when you're faced with a loss of vision. If it has already happened or begun to happen, in a way you are further along in your coping process because you don't have to wonder if perhaps there is a chance that you will be spared. In another way, though, you will never really come to grips with your vision loss if it seems to have stopped and then declines still further. According to Gail Handler, in an essay on coping with her own loss of vision to retinitis pigmentosa, "As the visual loss progresses, the patient may develop a feeling of being isolated from the normally sighted world while not completely comfortable in the sightless world." This state of limbo can cause your emotions to swing back and forth, making it feel like you're on a never-ending roller coaster ride.

On the other hand, the shock of a sudden and unexpected loss of vision can be more traumatic than knowing it's coming and having time to prepare. This is very similar to the difference between having a loved one die unexpectedly compared to seeing him or her decline and finally die after a long illness. When you know the death is coming, you can take the time to think of things you want to do before it happens, and you have time to get used to the idea and deal with the emotions that come with it. But you suffer along with the person while you wait for him or her to die, perhaps at times wondering if maybe he or she will beat it after all, and a lot of things in your life are put on hold in the meantime. Just as you grieve when a loved one dies, you will grieve the loss of your sight, and this grief process is something you must complete before you can reach the next stage, which is acceptance.

How you learn to accept your vision loss, and indeed whether you learn to accept it at all, will depend largely on your personality and how you have learned to cope with other losses or difficulties in your life. If you are a person with a basically negative outlook on life—if you reacted to the news of your disorder by thinking, "Well, this figures. Bad things always happen to me"—then you will probably have a hard time getting over your feelings of bitterness and anger at this latest turn of events in your life. If you are basically a positive person, you might still go through a stage of feeling cheated or pessimistic, wondering why you bother to look on the bright side when something like this is going to happen, but eventually your positive nature will return and your negative feelings will lessen. "When someone first loses sight, then he or she might be unhappy," the National Federation of the Blind asserts. "After receiving special help to learn how to do things as a blind person and having a more positive attitude about being blind, then a person can learn to feel okay about blindness."

Taking Control
When you have finally made peace with your vision disorder, you will be able to take control of how the disorder will fit into your life. Consider the stance taken by the National Federation of the Blind, which declares,

"The real problem of blindness is not the lack of eyesight. The real problem is the misunderstanding and lack of information that exist. If a blind person has proper training and opportunity, blindness is only a physical nuisance." Deciding how to handle all of the new challenges you now face and figuring out how to integrate this condition with the life you are accustomed to will require you to gather more knowledge and to do some creative thinking.

Begin by finding out as much as you can about your condition and also about what resources are available to you. Write down or tape-record questions for your eye doctor before your next appointment, and don't leave until you've gotten the answers. It can help to take someone along with you on the visit; afterward you can compare notes and see if what you heard the doctor say is the same as what the other person understood.

If you have health insurance, check with your insurer to learn what rehabilitation or training programs and equipment or low-vision aids the insurer will pay for. If the insurer's program does not provide much assistance in this area, ask if it will allow you to go outside the normal boundaries to obtain what you need.

Federal, state, and local government programs are another source for information, support, and supplies. Check your local telephone directory and ask your ophthalmologist or optometrist about programs for which you might qualify. Look into social service agencies and charitable groups in your area as well; many of these groups exist to help people with low or no vision. Your local library might also have resources for you, such as audiobooks, and

47

Questions to Ask Your Eye Care Professional

- ↝ What changes can I expect in my vision?

- ↝ Will my vision loss get worse? How much of my vision will I lose?

- ↝ Will regular eyeglasses improve my vision?

- ↝ What medical/surgical treatments are available for my condition?

- ↝ What can I do to protect or prolong my vision?

- ↝ Will diet, exercise, or other lifestyle changes help?

- ↝ If my vision can't be corrected, can you refer me to a specialist in low vision?

- ↝ Where can I get a low-vision examination and evaluation? Where can I get vision rehabilitation?

Questions to Ask Your Specialist in Low Vision

- ↝ How can I continue my normal, routine activities?

- ↝ Are there resources to help me in my job (or in school)?

- ↝ Will any special devices help me with daily activities like reading, sewing, cooking, or fixing things around the house?

- ↝ What training and services are available to help me live better and more safely with low vision?

- ↝ Where can I find individual or group support to cope with my vision loss?

the librarian might be able to steer you toward other programs that can provide further assistance.

The Internet can also be an important resource. Many of the groups that help visually impaired people have their own Web sites, and there are hundreds of sites devoted to every imaginable health condition. You should be able to find information on your vision disorder by searching the sites listed in the Where to Go for Help section of this book or elsewhere on the Web.

Knowing as much as you can about your condition, including what causes it, whether it is likely to progress, and what you can expect to experience in the near and far future, is much more empowering than avoiding the topic altogether. At first, some people don't want to know what is happening because they are afraid that the more they learn, the more fear they will have. Usually the opposite turns out to be true: Knowing what to expect, even if the outlook is not good, is less frightening than not knowing. Also, knowing what might happen gives you choices: If there are various treatment options, you can make an informed choice when you educate yourself about your condition. If your disorder is likely to get worse, you can make plans to prepare yourself before it happens, allowing you to begin to cope rather than experiencing devastating feelings of loss and grief with every stage of decline and giving you time to develop new strategies for managing your everyday tasks.

Developing New Skills

Many visually impaired people find it extremely helpful to take some classes or training from a facility or organization

Film Images: *A Patch of Blue*

A young woman (Elizabeth Hartman), blinded accidentally by her mother, is isolated by her blindness because no one has tried to help her learn about the world around her. When a kind businessman (Sidney Poitier) begins to teach her about the world she cannot see, she falls in love with him. She is white and unaware that he is black, and so her feelings are unaffected by racial prejudices, but her mother (Shelley Winters) is not so open-minded. For their roles in this film, Winters won an Academy Award, Hartman was nominated for an Oscar and won a Golden Globe, and Poitier was nominated for a Golden Globe. No rating; 1965.

that helps people with low vision or blindness. Learning to function without your sense of sight takes skill and practice; there is no need for you to learn everything the hard way when there are organizations and people who want to show you the many ways that other people have solved the problems you're facing and help you choose the best way for you. A mobility training program can help you learn ways to find your way around both inside and outside of your home. Other specialized training programs exist to show you techniques for cooking, managing your household, accomplishing grooming tasks like matching up outfits and shaving or putting on makeup, and going to school or work.

Some of the new skills you will need to develop as a person with a vision disorder are things that you already know how to do as a sighted person. It can be shocking to try to do something without your sense of sight that you've done a thousand times, seemingly without even being aware of it, let alone watching yourself do it. For example, climbing the stairs in your home, getting into a car, working the remote for the television or stereo, or folding clothes can all seem very different when you do them for the first time without your vision. So, while you learn new skills, you will also learn to take what you know about your old ways of doing things, and adapt that knowledge to invent new ways of managing the same tasks.

It might seem tempting sometimes to allow other people to do things for you. If you say you aren't sure how to do something, or if you hesitate or struggle with it, there will probably be someone there ready to take over for you. If you let them, people are very likely to become over-protective of you, and at first you might let them. After a while, though, you will probably want to do things for yourself so that you're not dependent on others. You will feel the need to show others that you can take care of yourself. When you begin to develop more confidence in your ability to live your life with low or no vision, you might become frustrated at not being allowed or encouraged to do things that you could do before. It is very common for sighted people to assume that visually impaired people have a much smaller repertoire of skills than they actually have. For this reason, you will often have to demand the opportunity to prove that you can do something. Developing a healthy balance of competence and confidence can help you to make opportunities for yourself in areas in which you really can grow and accomplish a lot.

Maximizing Your Education

In the United States, much effort has been made to allow blind and visually impaired children to attend regular schools. While it might be helpful to learn skills specifically for coping with blindness from a school for the blind, in most cases it is not necessary for a child to go to a special school for his or her entire education. There are many government-sponsored and privately funded programs that provide assistance for low-vision and blind students; in combination with flexibility and creativity on the part of the student, parents, and teachers, these programs can eliminate the roadblocks that in the past would have prevented visually impaired students from going to school with their sighted peers.

Don't be afraid to ask for what you need from your teachers, school administrators, and even your classmates. Your teacher can help you by giving you copies of the notes that he or she writes on the board and of any transparencies or slides that are shown in class. You can study these later, having someone read them to you while you transcribe them into braille or using voice-recognition software on your computer or a magnifier to read them yourself. Just being aware that there is a visually impaired person in the room can make people more aware of the way they talk; they might make a conscious effort to use words instead of gestures and to be more specific in what they say, for example, stating and repeating the words or figures that they are referencing instead of saying "this goes here and this goes with that." People might also react to your vision impairment by yelling at you as if you were deaf, but that's another topic (see Handling Difficult People later in this chapter).

As a student, someday soon you will need to start thinking about what you want to do when you graduate. Will you go to college? What kind of career do you want to have? Before you start to think that your choices will be very limited because of your vision disorder, listen to how the National Federation of the Blind answers the question "What kinds of jobs do blind people have?": "Just about anything . . . If you believe you can do the job, and if your employer believes you can, there are very few jobs blind people cannot do. It is most important for blind people to have the chance to choose whatever job they want, and for the public to give blind people the opportunity."

Knowing Your Rights

If you are legally blind, you should know that the law protects your right to go anywhere that the general public is allowed to go. According to the National Federation of the Blind, "Each state has a law that says blind people using canes or dogs have the same rights of public access as the sighted. This means that blind people can take their canes and dogs into public buildings, businesses, offices, restaurants, theaters, roller skating arenas, bowling alleys, amusement parks, on buses, trains, planes, and other public places. These laws were established from the work of the National Federation of the Blind to make sure that blind people have the same rights as everyone else."

It is also important for you to know that the law protects you against discrimination in the workplace. You cannot be denied a job just because of your vision impairment if you can show that you are able to perform the required duties. Even if the employer would have to make some changes, called "reasonable accommodations," in order to make it possible for you to work there, most employers cannot reject you because of this. (Some companies that are very small or have other special circumstances are exempt from this law.)

Dealing with Conditions Related to Your Vision Loss

If your low vision or blindness is due to a disease such as diabetes or cancer, you will still have more emotional work to do. Complications from diabetes can affect many other areas of your body in addition to threatening to make your vision even worse. Many people with diabetes try to ignore it, hoping that it will work itself out, and when complications arise they don't know what to do. Coping with a life-threatening disease like cancer is likely to make all of the emotional difficulties of dealing with the loss of vision even more painful and frightening. If you are facing a condition like this, please do look for and accept as much emotional support as you can find. It really can help to have people to talk to, whether they are experts in your condition or not. A network of supportive people who care about you can make all the difference in your recovery.

Handling Difficult People

Sighted people often don't know a lot about vision impairment. Many sighted people experience some discomfort when talking to or being around a person who has low vision or is blind; their minds are racing in an effort to think of what to say and, more important, what not to say. Sighted people who aren't used to interacting with blind people might speak louder to you; they do the same thing when talking to someone in a wheelchair. It makes no sense, but it's not something they do on purpose—it just seems to happen a lot.

Another hang-up a lot of sighted people seem to have is avoiding the words "see," "saw," "sight," "look," "blind," or anything else that refers to the sense of sight. This is similar to people avoiding references to death around someone who has just lost a loved one. Since words and expressions relating to vision are so common in our language, trying to avoid them when talking to a blind person will really put a damper on conversation. Blind people refer to "seeing" things, as in "I see that you've finished that project" or "look at this" or "let me see that." "Seeing" is not just a visual phenomenon.

You will probably have a lot of awkward, uncomfortable, or even comical experiences that are due to a sighted person's misunderstanding of what it's like to be you. The other person will probably be even more uncomfortable than you. You can make things easier by using humor to defuse a tense or awkward situation and let the other person know that it's okay for him or her not to know what to say or do. People will most likely be so relieved that you aren't hurt, angered, or offended by their ignorance that they will relax and act normal. There are other things that you can do to take the initiative and help people to be comfortable around you. Here are some ideas:

- When you meet someone or when someone new joins a conversation, put out your hand for a handshake and introduce yourself. This makes the other person comfortable because it avoids the person putting out his or her hand to shake, realizing that you can't see it, and then not knowing what to do to greet you. If you sense that someone new has walked in or joined your group, but the person hasn't spoken yet, don't assume the person is being rude by not identifying himself or herself; the person might feel that it would be interrupting. You can show that you are aware of his or her presence by leaning toward the person, putting out your hand, or saying a short "hi, who's there?" while still facing and listening to the person who is speaking to you.

- If someone offers you help that you don't need, say something like, "Thank you, but I'm okay for now. I'll let you know if I need you later." Smile and show that you appreciate the offer, even if you secretly feel defensive of your independence. If the person persists, perhaps by taking your arm as you cross a street, you can stop walking and say, nicely, "Actually, it makes it harder for me when you do that," or, "I appreciate your help, but I really do have to learn to do this on my own." Again, say it with a smile. Remember, most people just want to help in any way they can, and they don't realize everything you're capable of doing for yourself.

⮑ If you do want help—crossing a street or finding something on a store shelf, for example—just ask. The worst that can happen is the other person will say no or not respond, and that is rare. You can say something like, "I have trouble seeing. Could you show me where the tomato soup is?" or, "This street sounds pretty busy. Could you help me cross?" Then tell the person exactly how you want him or her to help, whether it's by guiding your hand to the right part of the shelf or handing the can directly to you, or by allowing you to hold the person's arm as you walk across the street. Be sure to say thank you, and if you add something like, "You did that just right," you'll make the person feel really good; remember that most sighted people don't encounter blind people in their daily lives, so being of help to you will most likely feel like an accomplishment to them.

⮑ Let people know what behaviors of theirs help or hinder your communication with them. For example, some people don't realize that it still matters that you look toward a blind person when you talk. Others don't think to let you know when they are leaving the room or walking away, and you can end up talking to the empty space where they used to be. If it would help you to have people write you notes using a certain color of ink or a thick marker, tell them. You could even buy each of your friends and family members one of the pens you prefer.

If you have low vision, you might sometimes encounter people who expect you to not be able to see anything at all and who doubt that you really have a vision disorder when they discover that you can see some things. This can even happen with people you know well. The National Association for Visually Handicapped notes that the fact that "your vision is impaired and you have trouble seeing but you are not blind" is "a difficult concept for many to comprehend." Some people might think you are faking it if you can sometimes see certain things, or if your vision fluctuates and allows you to see something one day but not the next.

If someone accuses you of not having a vision problem or of making it seem worse than it is in order to get sympathy or special treatment, it's up to you to decide how to respond. First, if there is any truth to the accusation, you don't have to admit it but you might want to examine the reasons why you are misrepresenting your condition. The Foundation Fighting Blindness reports that it can be a normal part of the adjustment process for newly blinded people to pretend they can see more or less than they really can. Even if the comment was made rudely or seemed to be intended to hurt you, you can use it as a heads-up to yourself to think about your feelings about your vision impairment.

If you have not misrepresented your condition and the person is someone whose opinion is important to you, or if the person is a teacher or supervisor whose assessment of you impacts your grades or career, you will probably want to make an effort to enlighten that person about your condition. A note from your ophthalmologist, mobility trainer, or other specialist involved in your treatment and rehabilitation might be all that is needed to refute the accusation. Make arrangements to sit down and talk to the person and explain the particulars of your condition. To someone who doesn't understand that your visual acuity can change from day to day and can be impacted by how sunny it is or how tired you are, seeing you do something on your own one time but ask for help the next time might seem like watching someone who is faking a limp and keeps switching legs. Try to remain calm and don't get defensive. Once you've explained your situation, the other person will probably feel bad about having accused you of using your vision impairment to your advantage, so try not to make it worse. If you really rub it in, that person might believe your explanation but will resent you for spotlighting their thoughtlessness.

If you go through the process of explaining your condition and the doubter still continues to accuse you of misrepresenting your visual abilities, you might want to talk to someone else, like the principal or your boss's boss. What the doubter is doing to you might be harassment. It is best to deal with a situation like this earlier rather than later; if you do not take action until after you have received a poor grade or performance review, it can be harder and more time-consuming to recover what you have lost. Also, it is better to bring a third person into a situation like this rather than make repeated attempts to set the other person straight on your own. If you've given it one good try and nothing has changed, find someone else to help you resolve the problem.

If the doubter is not someone in a position of power over you, you might decide to just ignore him or her. As you go through life, you will probably encounter people like this now and then. They're the same people who watch someone park in a handicapped parking space and assume that nothing is wrong with the person because he or she is able to walk into the store. Even if the doubter can see that the person has a handicapped parking permit, he or she will probably assume it was stolen or borrowed for the driver's convenience. These doubters don't think about the fact that handicapped parking permits are often issued for something that you can't see, like a heart condition or a breathing disorder. If you try to enlighten every person you encounter who is ignorant like this, you will succeed only in wasting a lot of time. People who want to confront you with their thoughts on your "claim" to be visually impaired aren't looking for an explanation: They're just looking for someone to pick on or fight with.

Some blind or low-vision people find it very rewarding to join organized groups for people with vision disorders. It can be a relief to spend time with people who have a basic understanding of the challenges you face and who will be able to relate to your experiences, both good and bad. On the other hand, some visually impaired people don't want to hang out with other visually impaired people, feeling that it is limiting, depressing, or even boring. Your opinion on the subject will probably depend on how you feel about your own vision disorder, whether or not you have accepted it, and the personalities of the people in the groups you might consider joining. If everyone just sits around feeling sorry for themselves, that group won't do you any good; but if you find one that includes people with positive attitudes and good advice to share, it can enrich your life in ways that nothing else can.

Tools and Techniques

Adapting your lifestyle to accommodate a severe vision disorder is a big job. It takes the learning of new skills, the acquisition of new ways of thinking, and a lot of creativity to make your life the way you want it to be. This chapter discusses issues affecting you at school and at work, including laws and organizations that are intended to help people with low vision or blindness by making sure opportunities are not denied to them and they are given the chance to use their abilities.

In this chapter you will also learn about dozens of techniques and tools that can help visually impaired and blind people to retain their independence. Some people avoid using low-vision aids at first because they don't want to appear to need special help. A better way to look at it, according to Barbara Freer in the *Voice of Dialogue*, is to see these tools as "symbols of independence—not as symbols of blindness." In some cases, a "blind" tool or technique might work better than a "low-vision" one, even if you have some sight. Therefore, these resources are not divided into "low-vision" and "blind" categories. If you have some vision, try to be creative in thinking of ways that your remaining vision can work for you and be realistic about what it can't do.

Also, think about the time and cost involved in using one tool or technique versus another. For example, you might find that having a talking or braille-numbered wrist-watch would be less expensive than a big-number clock in every room, and it would save you the time it takes to find a clock you can read if you're in a place where there are none. "One of the most important things a partially sighted person should learn," say Ruth Schroeder and Doris Willoughby of the National Federation of the Blind, "is that his or her sight is not efficient for certain things, and that a blind technique is superior in those instances."

Braille

The braille system, a method of reading and writing for blind people, is both a tool and a technique. It is named after Louis Braille, a French teacher of the blind who developed braille from a code system used by the army. It involves the use of raised dots on paper or other materials; these dots are read by touch. The braille dot alphabet consists of different combinations of the dots within a space, called a cell, that is two columns wide and three rows high. How the dots are arranged within each cell is what makes each letter, number, or punctuation mark. For example, the cell for the letter A contains one dot in the top left corner. Braille can also be used to transcribe music.

Whether or not you have some vision, learning braille can greatly increase your independence. While it might seem that relying on a method of communication that most people can't understand would serve only to isolate you even more, this is not the case. If you think of braille as a new language instead of as an admission of defeat, you will begin to see its usefulness. Using braille to communicate with others who can read it is no different from a sighted person using written notes, except that it is tactual (based on your sense of touch) instead of visual. Still, until you are unable to read at all using your remaining sight, you might not be very interested in learning braille. "To learn braille one must, I believe, have a deeply motivated desire to want to learn," wrote Gladys Loeb in an article entitled "Labeling with Braille." "It is my opinion therefore that there won't be a strong incentive to learn braille as long as a person can still read print."

While not everyone who loses their sight learns braille, most visually impaired people who do learn it find braille useful for at least some tasks. Children who are born blind or who lose their vision very early in life are usually taught braille in school or through special education programs. Reading braille can seem impossible on the first try, but eventually the little dots will begin to separate and make sense to you. Once you have learned the braille alphabet and the method for writing braille, you can make your own braille documents, either by hand or using a brailler, which is like a typewriter. People who are very accomplished with braille are able to take notes in braille in classes or meetings, and they can read braille as rapidly as a sighted person can read printed text. There are also a number of different devices that help people to read braille publications. These publications now can often be transcribed into "paperless" braille and read with a machine that electronically raises the dots in a panel as you read.

It used to be that braille had to be made one dot at a time with a punch and special heavy paper. This was obviously time-consuming and not practical for most applications. Now, however, in addition to the braille slate and punch method, braille labelers and typewriters are available and can be used to label items that do not come with braille markings already on them. You can make labels for canned and bottled items and other containers; cabinets and drawers; tools; knobs and handles; videos, cassette tapes, and CDs; and personal items. Braille labels are especially useful in the kitchen and bathroom. Braillers can be used to produce all of the same things as a regular typewriter, including letters, memos, lists, and other documents.

In addition to the braille conversions that you can make yourself, many of the items that are modified with bigger numbers, such as phones and calculators, are also manufactured in braille models. You can even make your own dots on various items using drops of paint, nail polish, glue, or even correction fluid, which now can be purchased in a pen that dispenses very small, precise drops.

Tools

The National Association for Visually Handicapped paints a grim picture of the availability of assistance for visually impaired people. "If you are visually impaired, that is, if you are among the majority of people with serious eye problems, you will find that the information and services available to you are sparse," the NAVH reports. As you read in chapter 6, getting people to understand the difference between low vision and blindness can be difficult, and so finding the right assistance for your needs may take more than one try.

There are a lot of products available for purchase in stores, by mail order, and on the Internet that might solve a problem you're having. Many of the organizations and Web sites listed in the Where to Go for Help section at the end of this book have a section or division devoted to low-vision aids. However, if you're clever you might be able to make your own product or modify something you already have to accomplish the same goal. Still, you should know what is available to you so that you can make an informed choice and understand that there are solutions to common problems faced by people with vision impairments.

Magnifiers

One of the biggest categories of low-vision aids is magnifiers. There are hundreds of different types with various magnification levels. In general, the larger magnifiers allow for greater levels of magnification than do the smaller ones. Some of the choices are:

➭ Handheld. There are dozens of different handheld magnifiers. Some look like a simple magnifying glass. Some can be folded and carried in your pocket or purse, or worn like a necklace around your neck. Some have a battery-operated light inside, which you can turn on to illuminate what you're reading and make it even easier to see. These magnifiers are useful for reading things like receipts, checks, bills, price tags, contracts, and package labels when you're out shopping or at a restaurant. They can also be used to read from a book or magazine.

☞ Hands-free. These are for reading that will take longer than it would be comfortable to hold a hand-held magnifier, or for times when you need to read or see something while doing something else with your hands. Some of these types of magnifiers sit on the page you're reading, and you move them over the lines as you read. Others are worn around your neck and are propped against your chest; you look down and through them to see. Some look like and are worn like goggles or glasses.

☞ Some medium-size models sit on a desk or table like a gooseneck lamp and are swung into position when needed. Some of these types of magnifiers come with a lamp; the magnifier and lamp can be used together or separately.

☞ Larger magnifiers look like computers and can be used for intensive reading or to allow for greater magnification than smaller models. Some have their own screens, while others project the image they scan onto a television screen. There are household and portable models of these magnifiers.

Big-Number and Big-Button Items

For people with reduced vision, sometimes all that is needed is for print to be bigger. A magnifier can accomplish this sometimes, but it is more convenient for the print to be already enlarged. To fill this need, there are large-print editions of books; watches, clocks, and timers with bigger numbers and wider hands; big-number playing cards and bingo cards; tape measures with a wider tape and larger numbers; phones, calculators, and remote control adapters with larger buttons; and even stick-on key enlargers for computer keyboards.

Talking and Voice-Recognition Items

There are a great number of products that can allow visually impaired people to take advantage of their sense of hearing to compensate for what they can no longer see. Examples of talking items include watches, clocks, bathroom scales, calculators, tape measures, and thermometers for taking your temperature or for the temperature outside. These items all recite the needed information when you activate them, for example, by pushing a button. Other products, such as phone dialers, are activated by a voice command. There are even labelers that allow you to record the contents of a container on a card and use it to label the container; when you've used what's inside the container, you can rerecord and reuse the label on something else. With some imagination, you can think of plenty of unique uses for devices like these.

One item that can be a big help to visually impaired people is a microcassette tape recorder. This handheld recorder can take the place of a daily planner, allowing the user to record "notes to self," to-do items, shopping lists, directions, appointments, and reminders. It can also be used to record lectures in school, eliminating the need for writing in a notebook. Many sighted students use microcassette recorders to tape lectures so they can pay attention to the lecture and not be distracted with trying to write everything down. There are also smaller versions of the microcassette recorder that do not use tapes and can be used to record short messages that you don't need to save. On the other hand, a larger tape recorder might make sense to use for school because it takes regular cassette tapes, which can then be played back in a home or car stereo. There is no need to go to a low-vision aids source for these recorders: They are all available in regular department and electronics stores.

Lamps and Lights

Sometimes a person with low vision can see what they want to see if there is the right type and amount of light. For this reason, special lamps and lights that provide more direct, intense light than a typical lamp are available through low-vision aids catalogs. There are floor-size models as well as ones for the table or desktop, and even small flashlights that you can carry with you and use when you need more light at school, in a restaurant, or in a car.

General lighting in the home and at work is also important. In some cases, increasing lighting can make certain areas safer, such as stairways, landings, and closets. Lights can be mounted along stair railings, under cabinets in the kitchen and bathroom or at your desk, inside closets, and outside along the borders of sidewalks or paths. Many types of lights are solar-powered or run on batteries, so they do not require any wiring.

In other cases, reducing bright light, such as direct sunlight and glare from the sun, fluorescent light fixtures, and bright lamps can increase comfort and visual acuity. You can use drapes or blinds to control the amount of light coming through the windows, and you can arrange the furniture in a room so that your back will be to the glare when you sit. A glare screen on your computer can make using it more comfortable for you.

Motion sensors that turn lights on when you approach and turn them off after a certain amount of time can be very helpful because they prevent you from fumbling for light switches or cords.

One important thing to remember about lighting is that you are not going to damage your sight further by trying to read or use your remaining sight in low light. "It is disheartening to be told that it is dangerous to read in dim light, when brighter light is often uncomfortable, or that 'you must save your sight,'" says Lorraine Marchi, founder and executive director of the National Association for Visually Handicapped. "In fact, the more a visually limited person uses remaining vision, the better that person will be able to see."

Reading and Writing Aids

One of the most carefully guarded abilities for most visually impaired people is the ability to read and write. Braille was developed for this reason, but most people want to retain the ability to read regular print and to write in the usual way, either by hand or with a computer. Magnifiers are one of the biggest components of this category of aid, as are large-print editions of regular books, but there are many others as well. These include paper that is printed with dark lines to make it easier to write straight; writing templates for checks, envelopes, and letters that have cutouts to show you the places where you need to write; single-line highlighters and line-at-a-time reading templates that help to separate small portions of printed text for you to concentrate on as you read; and big-print address books, calendars, and other organization and time-management tools.

Another popular type of tool for reading is the reading machine or reading software for your computer. Because reading braille can be a rather slow process, some people prefer to use reading machines that scan the text of regular publications and feed the data into a computer that converts it into synthesized spoken words. When they are available, many people also make use of audiobooks and recordings that are made specifically for visually impaired people by assisting organizations. Through these organizations, visually impaired people have access to newspapers, magazines, textbooks, and novels on tape.

Dog Guides

Some low-vision and blind people use dog guides, also known as Seeing Eye dogs or Leader Dogs, to retain their independence. This program is not for everyone, though; some people are satisfied with using a cane or rely on the tactile information it provides, information that would not be available with a dog. Also, some people are not suited to being a dog-guide owner; they may not have the mobility skills needed to direct the dog properly, or they may not have the temperament needed to be half of a successful person/dog guide team. Those who do want to have a dog guide must complete a training program, learn to work with the dog that is chosen for them, and be able and willing to care for the dog.

For those for whom a dog guide is a good match, the program can open new doors and provide greater mobility and freedom. According to Leader Dogs for the Blind, having a dog guide "may minimize the difficulties of blindness and permit an individual to go where he or she wants to go—when he or she wants to go—without having to wait for a relative or friend. It will permit travel freedom, provide constant companionship, and widen the scope for job opportunity. A Leader Dog protects against everyday travel hazards and provides safety under trying conditions." Leader Dogs for the Blind is one of many organizations that train dogs to work as guides for visually impaired masters at little or no cost to the new owner (see Where to Go for Help). Dog guides are allowed by law to accompany their owners to work and in public places, even those that prohibit other dogs.

Human Resources

Perhaps the most important resource available to a visually impaired person is other people. If you have low vision or are blind, it is important for you to learn to do as much for yourself as you can, but it is also important for you to know when to ask for help. There will be times when it would be time-consuming, dangerous, or nearly impossible for you to do something yourself, and it would make more sense for you to make use of the network of people who are willing to help you. These might include family, friends, teachers, coworkers, and agencies that provide various types of assistance for visually impaired clients.

➭ Assistants. In some cases, a student may be able to obtain an assistant to accompany him or her to school. The person might be a volunteer or someone who is paid through a government-funded program, a charitable organization, a private foundation, or other means. This person can reduce the burden on the teacher to make needed accommodations for the student by taking notes or clarifying items that are presented visually but not verbally.

☞ Teachers. Teachers can help by giving visually impaired students copies of transparencies or of what they will write on the board before class starts so students who cannot easily take notes can follow the discussion and study later. They can also be aware of how often they make reference to things that the sighted students can see and learn to adapt their way of lecturing to explain the visual elements for their visually impaired students.

☞ Eyecare specialists. The person who helps you with your vision might have one of three titles: optician, optometrist, or ophthalmologist. An ophthalmologist is a true "eye doctor" who can test your eyes and prescribe glasses or contacts, diagnose and treat diseases, and even perform surgery on your eyes if needed. An optometrist is not a medical doctor, but has graduated from a school of optometry and can test your vision and prescribe glasses or contacts. An optometrist can also detect signs of disease in the eye and can alert you to see an ophthalmologist when needed. An optician is the person who fills the prescriptions for corrective lenses—glasses or contacts—written by optometrists and ophthalmologists.

An optician creates the lenses for your glasses and fits them into the frames, or makes sure that you get contact lenses that correct your vision and fit the unique shape of your eyeball according to the prescription, but does not examine your eyes or test your vision.

These are the three types of eyecare specialist that a person with normal vision or mild to moderate problems is likely to encounter. If you have a disorder that affects your vision in a moderate to severe way, however, you might find that you need a vision rehabilitation specialist. If your regular eye doctor has done everything he or she can but you are still limited by low vision, a vision rehabilitation specialist might be able to go further. This specialist can prescribe low-vision aids such as magnifiers, telescopic devices, closed-circuit televisions, and other equipment to further enhance your remaining vision. He or she may also be able to offer suggestions for techniques, support groups, and other resources to help you deal with your low vision. Your regular eye doctor should be able to give you the name of a vision rehabilitation specialist in your area.

⮑ Trainers. Mobility specialists, rehabilitation therapists, and trainers for the visually impaired can be a great help to a person who is newly blind or even to people whose sight has gradually deteriorated to the point where they can no longer do something significant, such as reading or cooking. If you have exhausted your ideas for adapting sighted techniques to your needs as a person with low vision, you might want to think about

73

working with one of these specialists or taking a class in mobility and independence techniques. Learning a new skill to replace one that you have had to give up can give you a new lease on life and a big boost in self-esteem.

Techniques

People who have lost or are gradually losing their sight have to learn to adapt to living and working in an environment that seemed much safer and easier to maneuver when they could see. This adaptation process can be made easier through education, mobility training, talking to other visually impaired people, and creative thinking by you and your friends and family.

The adaptations you make will depend on the particular circumstances of your vision loss. For example, if you have macular degeneration, you will learn to make the most of your peripheral vision. Where as in the past your peripheral vision was used mostly to give you supporting information for your central vision, now it is your primary way of seeing. You (and your brain) will have to adapt to this change.

You can experiment with the various low-vision aids on the market, including magnifiers and reading machines, and you will quickly discover which ones will help you. A technique that is recommended specifically for people with macular degeneration is to try using a mirror to direct images from the center of your field of vision into your peripheral vision so that you can see them.

With some experimentation and a positive attitude, you will find ways to work around the disabled portion of your vision and make the most of your remaining vision. If you have no remaining vision, mobility training and, again, creative thinking and brainstorming between you and your support group can make a significant impact on your independence, happiness level, and quality of life.

Film Images: *Scent of a Woman*

In this award-winning film, an abrasive, alcoholic, blind retired army colonel (Al Pacino) teaches a young prep school student (Chris O'Donnell) about the important things in life. Pacino earned an Oscar and a Golden Globe for his performance, and the film earned an Oscar nomination and the Golden Globe Award for Best Drama. R; 1992.

Get Organized

An organized approach to daily life is much more rewarding than being surrounded by chaos and always worrying about being late for appointments. This is true of all people, sighted or sightless. However, since people rely on their vision to provide them with 80 percent of the information they process every day, being organized becomes even more important when you lose your sight.

If you are already an organized person who has systems and strategies in place for things like doing homework, cleaning your room, cooking, or doing chores, then you will probably have an easier time reorganizing those patterns for life with low vision or blindness. If you are naturally disorganized, however, the time has come for you to change that tendency. Working with an orientation/mobility specialist can help you to come up with systems that will allow you to accomplish the things you need to do in the safest and least time-consuming way possible. These specialists will often come to your home and actually show you how to rearrange things, how to use what you already have, or how to add a few specialized items to make adapting to your vision disorder as easy as possible.

Another option is hiring a professional organizer, a person who specializes in helping people to get organized, whether it's arranging closets and cabinets, honing time-management skills, or handling paperwork, filing, and other regular tasks. Some professional organizers specialize in working with people with impaired vision. You can contact the National Association of Professional Organizers for a referral to an organizer near you (see Where to Go for Help).

Below are just a few tips for accomplishing everyday tasks. These techniques all involve your sense of touch, and the principles behind them can be applied to all areas of your life. The Foundation Fighting Blindness says, "Touch everything! The sense of touch is a most valuable tool, but it must be trained and encouraged. Substituting touch for vision does not 'come naturally' to most people. But it will come with training and patience." Read through these ideas and then think of other ways you can use touch in place of sight.

Labeling Containers

Braille is a very useful way to label containers. You can use a braille labeler and attach the labels to small cards that you then rubber-band around the containers, allowing you to reuse the labels. In her essay "Labelling with Braille," Gladys Loeb recommends using pinking shears, which are scissors that cut a zig-zag instead of a straight line, to cut the top edges of your labels so you will be able to tell easily which way is up. If you do the grocery shopping in your household, you can take labels with you to the store for the things you intend to buy and that you cannot identify by touch, the sound they make, or other means. As the bagger is bagging your items, have him or her attach your labels to the containers for you. Then when you get home you can put them away where they belong without waiting for someone to help you identify them. In addition to labels, you can use various combinations of rubber bands, ribbons, clips, or glued-on small objects with distinctive shapes to identify cans, bottles, jars, and other containers.

Once you have experimented a little bit with labeling, you will probably start to see hundreds of uses for this technique. Even if you don't know braille, you can still come up with labeling methods that use the rubber bands and other attaching devices or the distinctive items that you can attach to identify something or distinguish it from other, similar items.

Identifying Clothes

Often you will be able to distinguish different types of clothing based on the feel of the material. For example, jeans have a distinctive feel, and so does silk. You should have no problem telling towels apart from clothes. Some things can be identified by the overall shape of the item, especially undergarments, or by the shape of some part of it, such as the buttons or other fasteners or any decorative appliques or stitching.

If you have some items that feel alike, or that are the same item in different colors, you can use a number of different techniques to tell them apart. You can attach safety pins to the labels or inside seams, thinking of a meaning for each size or number of pins, or putting small beads or buttons on the pins to give yourself even more different options.

You could also cut off a portion of the label inside the item and give it a shape that you will remember and associate with that particular piece, or you could devise a system where you make a cut into the label from any of the sides and at varying angles, with each cut indicating something different. For example, a notch cut into the left side of the label that angles toward the top of the label could indicate a red item; a cut in the same position that goes straight across means the item is orange, while a cut in the same position but angling down means it is yellow, and so on. You can also use any of these techniques to identify different household members' clothes if you are responsible for doing everyone's laundry.

Another handy trick for keeping paired items like socks together is to clip them with a clothespin or a sock holder ring as soon as you take them off. This way you only have to pair them up once; from then on they will always be together, whether they are on your feet or not. Again, if you do everyone's laundry, this technique can save a lot of time. Ask everyone to get in the habit of clipping their socks together before they throw them into the hamper or laundry chute.

Attaching safety pins and other fasteners or clips to various items can help you to identify lots of things besides clothes. Think of some other ways that you can use safety pins, paper clips, binder clips, clothespins, or other fasteners.

Sorting Money

Sorting coins is fairly simple because they all feel different, either in size or in whether their edges are smooth or ridged. Sorting paper money, which is all the same size, weight, and color (in the United States), can seem trickier until you learn the many uses of folding. You can decide how you will handle each type of bill—any way that works is fine. For example, you might fold your singles into fourths, your fives in half the short way, your tens in half the long way, and leave your twenties unfolded. This way you know what each bill is and you can be confident that you are paying with the right one. It is probably a good idea to try to pay with exact change whenever possible, so that you don't have to deal with getting change back and figuring out what denominations you've received. Of course, many transactions are now done with credit or debit cards, eliminating the need for you to deal with cash at all.

Folding strategies can be used whenever you need to keep track of any type of paper. You can probably think of dozens or even hundreds of applications for various folding methods.

Safety Issues

One of the most important, and most frightening, things about losing your sight is that there are now new dangers for you to contend with in daily life. If you lose your sight completely, you will probably have some painful trips, bumps, falls, burns, or other accidents as you learn to navigate without the use of your eyesight. If your vision gradually deteriorates, you may have a chance to get used to it slowly, and if the prognosis of your condition is that it is likely to get worse as time goes on, you can begin to think of how you will continue to adapt your systems to your changing needs.

While it is important for your self-esteem and happiness that you retain as much of your independence as possible, it is also important for your safety and the safety of others that you learn to recognize and accept your limits. Do practice doing things for yourself instead of allowing others to always "let me do that for you." After all, if you don't try you will never learn. However, if you stubbornly insist on doing things that are dangerous for anyone with impaired vision, such as driving, or if you continue to do things the way you used to do them without learning and practicing safe sightless adaptations, such as running down stairs, using knives, or cooking, you run the risk of harming yourself and those around you. Perhaps worst of all, you will make people doubt your judgment, and they will either refuse to help you at all or they will refuse to let you do anything for yourself.

It is best to begin slowly and work on developing safe habits while building your skills and learning to rely more heavily on your other senses. Think creatively and figure out ways to solve the new problems confronting you, but be sure to think through your ideas instead of just leaping into them. In the beginning you might need to also rely on other people much more than you really want to. Just keep in mind that your skills will increase—you will learn to do things for yourself that sighted people will find amazing—and eventually you will become much less dependent on others for your everyday needs. When the time comes to take back some of the control that you have had to give to others, they will give it up much more easily if they see that you are careful and do not take unnecessary risks.

Kitchen Tasks

One of the most dangerous places for a person with low or no vision is the kitchen. Even if you are not the one cooking, you must be very careful and aware of your surroundings so that you don't knock a pot of hot food or liquid off the stove, cut yourself on a knife left on the counter, or bump into something breakable. Even finding something to eat that doesn't require cooking can be dangerous if nonfood items such as cleaning supplies are kept in the same cabinets with foods.

Using the oven and stove can cause problems for people with impaired vision. Some people recommend using an electric stove, because the open flame of a gas stove is more likely to start a fire if you drape your sleeve or a potholder in it. Stirring a pot on the stove can be tricky, but there are devices available from low-vision aids suppliers that help keep the pot centered on the burner and hold the handle steady so you can stir one-handed. Also, reaching into a hot oven can be very dangerous, so it is recommended that you pull the oven shelf out and remove the item from it rather than reaching into the oven to retrieve it.

There are a lot of low-vision aids that can help you to work safely in the kitchen. For example, how do you pour a beverage into a cup or glass without it overflowing? Many people use their finger to gauge when the liquid has reached almost to the top. This can be okay when you're pouring your own drink, but others probably don't want your fingers in their beverages. Also, this method is a pretty painful way to pour hot drinks like coffee. The solution is to use a liquid level indicator, a small device that hangs over the edge of the cup or glass and makes a sound when the drink reaches almost to the top. In time, you will probably learn to gauge the amount that your favorite glasses and cups will hold, and you will be able to fill them by timing how long you pour, feeling the weight of the container, and listening to the change in the sound of the liquid when the container is almost full. If you need to make a certain amount of boiling water, it is best to measure the water while it is still cold and then boil it. If you use it right when it starts to boil, you won't lose very much to evaporation.

Besides the low-vision aids available from catalogs, Web sites, and suppliers, there are also a lot of things that you can buy in regular stores and adapt for your needs. For example, some timers have raised numbers on them that make them suitable for use by people with low vision.

Despite all of the equipment, tools, and tips available to help a visually impaired person work in the kitchen, the most important ingredient is confidence. As Ruth Schroeder and Doris Willoughby say in their article "Suggestions for the Blind Cook," published by the National Federation of the Blind, "A positive attitude is essential to success. If you really believe that the blind cook necessarily takes many safety risks, needs a great deal of special equipment, has only a limited repertoire, and produces questionable products, then you will do a poor job. If you really believe that the blind cook may choose among many good methods to work with all kinds of food and produce high-quality products, then you will find a way to succeed."

Taking Medication

Just as it is important for you to know that what you are ingesting in the kitchen is pudding and not silver polish, or Parmesan cheese and not drain cleaning crystals, it is also very important that you come up with a foolproof system for taking medicines. Again, discuss this with everyone in the household. You can brainstorm for ideas, and you can also make sure that everyone understands how important it is not to move or switch medicine bottles once you have a system in place.

Working with Electricity

We've all been told never to touch an electrical outlet or stick anything other than a plug into it. So, if you can't see the outlet and you have begun to rely on your hands to find things, how can you safely plug something in? You can use your hands to find the outlet, and even to position the prongs on the plug; the trick is to go slowly and be very careful. If you use your fingers to line up the prongs with the slots in the outlet, just make sure that your hands are not wet and that you take your fingers away from the plug before you begin to push it into the outlet. When unplugging an item, take the extra time to trace the cord all the way to the wall so that you can remove the plug by grasping the plug itself, not just by pulling on the cord. This will prevent damage to the cord, such as separation of the plug from the body of the cord. Similarly, before you plug something in, feel the length of the cord and area around the plug to find any frayed areas or exposed portions of the wire. If you find any of these flaws, do not plug the item in.

Household Maneuvering

Standing or sitting in one place in your familiar home is one way to ensure that you won't trip over something, fall down a set of stairs, or slam your head into an obstacle. But sitting or standing still won't get you anywhere; sooner or later, you'll have to learn how to move safely through your home, and eventually through the unfamiliar world outside.

If you live with sighted people, you will all have to learn the modifications that are needed in order for the home to be safe for the visually impaired member of the family. One of the most important rules is that nothing should ever be left on the floor where you might trip on it. This is even more important in areas at the top of stairs or on landings, where a trip or fall could cause serious injury. Another important rule, and one that you might not think of immediately, is how to handle doors. Everyone in the household will have to reach an agreement on this point and then stick to it. In general, entryway and interior room doors should be left either closed or opened all the way, flat against the wall, to prevent the visually impaired person from walking into them and suffering an injury to the head, face, knee, or shoulder. Doors on cabinets should be kept closed.

Once you begin to think about the placement and positioning of things, you will realize that if you make it a policy to keep things in the same place whenever possible, your shins will have a lot fewer bruises and you will have fewer broken household items. You will need to make decisions about where to position each piece of furniture, including dining room chairs, footstools, and other items that are usually moved around somewhat. Examine what, if anything, is likely to be found on the furniture, including blankets, toss pillows, remote controls, newspapers, and even pets. Nothing that could be broken from being sat on should be left in a place that is meant for sitting.

Speaking of pets, you might find that putting a bell on each pet will prevent some trips and unintended kicks if your little friend is in your path when you are walking through the home. A bell can also help you to locate your pet if you need to, for example, to take him or her to the vet. Some people even put bells on their small children to keep from tripping over them and to keep track of their whereabouts when they start taking crawling, toddling, or climbing expeditions around the house.

Also consider items that are usually found on tables, such as candles, vases, or statues. It is best to keep these things to a minimum, since the possibility of breaking them either by knocking them over or causing them to fall if you bump into the table increases when you have a lot of them out. You might also consider using a product like Museum Putty, which is a clear, sticky substance used to secure small collectibles to shelves or tabletops.

As if just walking around didn't present enough challenges, another move that can leave a bruise is bending down, according to Gladys Loeb in an article on home safety for visually impaired people. Obstacles that you might not feel when you're standing straight up, such as tabletops and chairs, can reach out and knock you in the head when you bend down. Says Loeb, "I'll never forget a close call I had in doing my laundry one day. I misjudged my location with respect to the concrete laundry tub... My hair brushed against the sharp corner and I shudder to think of what would have happened had I been an inch closer."

While it may seem challenging to get everything in your home set up just right, that's nothing compared to maneuvering in public. Once you venture out into the world beyond your home, you will most likely choose either a cane or a dog to help you find your way. The red-tipped white cane is a device that just about everyone knows is used by blind people to feel curbs, sidewalks, doorways, steps, and any obstacles in their path before they reach them. The cane is long enough to extend about two steps ahead of you, allowing you to move around obstacles in your way and step up or down as needed. A dog guide is another method of maneuvering around obstacles. One common misconception about dog guides is that they know when it is safe for their owners to cross a street. The truth is that the owner must listen to the traffic and determine when it is safe to cross, at that point giving the dog the command to move forward. If the dog senses that it is not safe, he or she will refuse to obey, but this is not the same as deciding for the owner when to move. For the visually impaired person, the ability to judge traffic by sound is one of many skills that must be learned in order to navigate the world safely.

Personal Safety

Quite often sighted people take a lot of chances with their personal safety without even realizing it, but when you lose your sight, you can feel very vulnerable and worry more about being mugged or attacked. As in other areas of your life, you can learn to rely on your other senses to keep yourself safe. As you begin to fine-tune the use of your senses of hearing, smell, touch, and even taste, you can gather important clues about your surroundings and the people near you. According to the Foundation

Film Images: *The Miracle Worker*

The classic true story of Helen Keller, blind, deaf, and mute since infancy, and Anne Sullivan, the teacher who breaks through her barriers and helps her to learn to communicate. In the original film version, Anne Bancroft played Sullivan and Patty Duke played Keller, and both received Oscars for their performances; a later made-for-television version features Duke as the teacher and Melissa Gilbert as Keller. No rating; 1962 and 1979.

Fighting Blindness, "The sense of touch and hearing remain as they were before the loss of sight. The only difference is that people who cannot see well practice using abilities that previously were used less because sight was used instead." You will learn what sounds, smells, and even air temperatures are normal in familiar situations; your awareness of your surroundings will increase in certain ways, for example, in knowing the correct or normal positioning of furniture, doors, windows, and items on tables, shelves, countertops, and windowsills. Just as a sighted person can enter his or her home and sense that something is wrong, realizing only later that it was a door out of position or an unfamiliar smell in the air, a visually impaired person can do the same things. Still, it can take time to get used to the idea that you can't just look around to gauge the safety of your situation. In time, though, your comfort level and confidence will increase.

All of the same basic rules of personal safety apply to visually impaired people. These include confirming the identity of a person at the door before you open it; refusing to give personal information to a caller whom you don't know; carrying your wallet in a front inside pocket instead of a back pocket or purse whenever possible; not getting into a vehicle with someone you don't know; keeping your doors locked when you are at home or in a vehicle; and being alert to what is happening around you wherever you are and whatever you are doing.

Your intuition, or "sixth sense," about a situation is often your most valuable self-defense mechanism, whether you have perfect vision or none at all. If you feel nervous, anxious, or afraid, even if there seems to be no good reason for you to feel this way, it is best to listen to your intuition and get out of the situation as quickly as possible. Gavin de Becker, an authority on personal safety, explains this concept in his book *The Gift of Fear*. He describes intuition as "knowing without knowing why." If it seems, however, that you are always on alert and waiting for something bad to happen, your intuition won't be able to warn you of real danger—you won't be able to hear it over the constant worry and fear you're feeling. "I strongly recommend caution and precaution," says de Becker, "but many people believe—and we are even taught—that we must be extra alert to be safe. In fact, this usually decreases the likelihood of perceiving hazard and thus reduces safety." It is when you can learn to be attentive without being nervous all the time, paying "relaxed attention" to your environment, that your intuition will serve you well.

How you evaluate other people can change when you lose your vision. Sighted people rely heavily on facial expressions and the overall "look" of a person to determine his or her intentions and whether or not the person should be trusted. For this reason, it can be very disconcerting to try to "judge" a person if you can't see his or her face. Still, when you learn to use your other senses, you might do an excellent job of evaluating people's intentions or the truthfulness of what they're saying when seeing them might have just confused you. It may be easier to identify inconsistencies in what is being said when you can't see the facial expressions or body movements that the person is using as he or she speaks. Most of the time, you won't analyze every word a person says to you, but sometimes something the person says will get your attention and your intuition will send you a message. Says de Becker, "We intuitively evaluate people all the time, quite attentively, but they only get our conscious attention when there is a reason. We see it all, but we edit out most of it. Thus, when something does call out to us, we ought to pay attention."

As you adapt to your vision loss, you might go through a stage of excessive worry and anxiety during which you think that every criminal can see that you are a sitting duck. This can, unfortunately, become a self-fulfilling prophecy: If you look like a victim, you are more likely to be chosen as one. People who appear confident and aware of their surroundings are less desirable as targets for purse-snatching or mugging because they look like they could put up a fight, scream, run, or do something else to complicate the robbery. People who walk with their heads down, who look like they don't know where they are going, or who appear to be lost in thought are more likely to be victimized. Any time you are out in public, for example, walking down a sidewalk or shopping in a mall, be aware of how you look to other people. Try to be aware of what's happening around you, walk as if you have somewhere to go and you know exactly where it is, and keep your head up to show that you are confident and you are paying attention. These tips can't guarantee that you will never be the victim of a crime, but research has shown that not acting like a victim improves your odds of never becoming one.

Eventually your initial fears will most likely lessen and you will return to a state of comfort in your environment. It is at this point that your intuition will be able to do its job. When you feel uncomfortable in a situation, even if

Film Images: *Ice Castles*

A young figure skater training for the Olympics (Lynn-Holly Johnson) loses most of her sight in an accident on the ice, but with the help of her boyfriend (Robby Benson), she learns to work around her disability and return to competition. PG; 1979.

you can't find a reason for it, says de Becker, "trust that what causes alarm probably should, because when it comes to danger, intuition is always right in at least two important ways: It is always in response to something [and] it always has your best interest at heart."

It's All in the Attitude

In this book you've learned about some methods for dealing with the mechanics of vision disorders and also the emotions that go with losing your sight. After this chapter you will find sections directing you to even more information and resources.

It is normal and even necessary to go through a period of grieving in which you mourn the loss of your visual ability. Eventually, though, you need to move on. Treat your condition as a challenge and learn to make the most of what you have, both any remaining sight you might have and the life you have in front of you.

Glossary

amblyopia   A condition that can result from strabismus, in which one eye is weaker than the other and needs to be forced to work correctly.

astigmatism   A problem caused by an uneven cornea surface, which can affect how well you see.

biofeedback   A type of therapy in which you learn to control unconscious or involuntary bodily functions, such as the eye movements of strabismus.

braille   A system of raised dots that is read by blind people, using their fingers to feel the dots instead of seeing letters with their eyes.

cataract   When the lens of an eye becomes cloudy.

ciliary processes   The structures within the eye that produce the vitreous fluid contained in the eyeball.

color blindness   The common term for color vision deficiency, in which a person is unable to tell certain colors apart.

cone cells   The cells in the retina that are responsible for "reading" both light and color.

conjunctivitis   A common eye infection also known as pink eye.

cornea   The front layer of the eye.

depth perception   The ability that allows you to catch a ball or reach for and pick up an object. You must have the use of both eyes to have depth perception.

diabetes   A disease that can cause serious complications in many parts of the body, including the eyes, and can lead to blindness.

diabetic retinopathy The complication of diabetes that can damage the retinas and cause blindness.

eyeguards Protective eyewear, which should always be worn when playing sports or working with tools or chemicals.

farsightedness A vision problem that prevents the person from clearly seeing things close-up.

fovea An area of the retina that is affected by albinism.

glaucoma A disease that causes increased pressure within the eye, which can lead to blindness.

hyperopia One form of farsightedness.

hypertension The formal name for high blood pressure, which can cause eye problems.

iris The colored part of the eye.

lazy eye The common term for amblyopia.

lens The middle part of the eye through which light comes in.

macula The portion of the retina that allows you to see fine detail.

macular degeneration A condition in which the macula breaks down, causing a person to lose sight in the center of his or her field of vision.

melanoma A form of cancer that sometimes occurs in the eyes.

monocular Something that affects or involves only one eye.

myopia The formal name for nearsightedness.

nearsightedness A vision problem that prevents a person from clearly seeing things from a distance.

ophthalmologist A medical doctor who examines the eyes, performs surgery, and prescribes corrective lenses.

optician A specialist who fills prescriptions for glasses and contact lenses.

optometrist A specialist who prescribes corrective lenses.

papilledema Atrophy or death of the optic nerve, caused by excessive pressure inside the skull.

peripheral vision   The top, bottom, and sides of a person's field of vision.

presbyopia   One form of farsightedness.

radial keratotomy   A surgical procedure used to correct nearsightedness.

retina   The back inside lining of the eye, on which images are focused.

retinitis pigmentosa   A hereditary condition that causes the retina to break down and can result in tunnel vision.

retinoblastoma   A form of cancer of the eye.

rod cells   Cells in the retina that "read" light coming into the eye.

strabismus   A condition in which the eyes do not work together, causing crossed eyes or other misalignments.

tactual   Related to the sense of touch.

trabecular meshwork   The area of the eye that allows the vitreous fluid to drain away.

tunnel vision   Being able to see only a small area straight ahead and in the center of the field of vision.

Where to Go for Help

In the United States

AMD Alliance International
11460 Johns Creek Parkway
Duluth, GA 30097
(877) 263-7171
Web site: http://www.amdalliance.org
An international nonprofit organization that works to raise awareness of age-related macular degeneration (AMD). The Web site includes a chart called the Amsler Grid, which can in some cases point out changes in vision that could be early symptoms of AMD.

American Council of the Blind
1155 15th Street NW
Suite 1004
Washington, DC 20005
(800) 424-8666
Web site: http://www.acb.org
This organization strives to improve the well-being of all blind and visually impaired people. Its services include a free monthly newsletter published in braille, large-print, cassette, and computer diskette formats. Its Web site includes information on guide dogs, braille publications, and other resources.

American Foundation for the Blind
11 Penn Plaza
Suite 300
New York, NY 10001
(800) 232-5463
Web site: http://www.afb.org
E-mail: afbinfo@afb.net
Maintains a directory of low-vision clinics throughout the
United States.

American Printing House for the Blind
P.O. Box 6085
Louisville, KY 40206-0085
(502) 895-2405
(800) 223-1839
Web site: http://www.aph.org
The APH publishes braille books and teaching aids for teach-
ers working with blind students. A free catalog is available.

American Society of Cataract and Refractive Surgery/American
Society of Ophthalmic Administrators
4000 Legato Road, Suite 850
Fairfax, VA 22033
(703) 591-2220
Web site: http://www.ascrs.org
The Web site of the ASCRS/ASOA provides detailed information about the surgical techniques currently used to correct
refractive errors and remove cataracts.

Assistive Media
400 Maynard Street
Suite 404
Ann Arbor, MI 48104-2434
(734) 332-0369

Web site: http://www.assistivemedia.org
This organization's mission is "to produce spoken-word inter-
pretations of literary works to serve persons with disabilities.
These recordings are to be made easily accessible and always
free-of-charge via the Internet."

Choice Magazine Listening
85 Channel Drive
Port Washington, NY 11050
(516) 883-8280
Web site:
http://www.geocities.com/Heartland/6056/choicemagazine.html
A free service that provides audiotapes of current magazine
articles to people who are blind, visually impaired, or unable
to read because of other physical limitations.

Dynamic Living
(888) 940-0605
Web site: http://www.dynamic-living.com
This Web site offers products enabling people with disabilities
to maintain their independence. Includes a "Blind/Low
Vision" section.

Foundation Fighting Blindness
Executive Plaza I, Suite 800
11350 McCormick Road
Hunt Valley, MD 21031-1014
(800) 394-3937
(800) 683-5551 (TDD)
Web site: http://www.blindness.org
A national eye research organization that funds retinal degen-
erative disease research in the United States and foreign coun-
tries and also serves as a source of information for eye care
specialists, professionals, and affected families. The Web site

includes tips on changing your Internet settings to make Web pages easier to read and features several very informative articles by Gladys Loeb covering topics such as safety, braille labeling, and kitchen organization.

Guide Dogs for the Blind Inc.
P.O. Box 151200
San Rafael, CA 94915-1200
(800) 295-4050
Web site: http://www.guidedogs.com
A nonprofit organization that provides guide dogs and training for recipients at no cost.

Leader Dogs for the Blind
P.O. Box 5000
Rochester, MI 48308
(888) 777-5332
Web site: http://www.leaderdog.org
This organization provides dog guides and training for the legally blind.

National Alliance for Eye and Vision Research
426 C Street NE
Washington, DC 20002
(202) 544-1880
Web site: http://www.eyeresearch.org
A nonprofit organization that works to further eye and vision research and to educate the public about eye and vision issues. The Web site offers research information and tips for contacting elected officials to encourage them to fund further research.

National Association for Visually Handicapped
22 West 21st Street
New York, NY 10010

(212) 889-3141
Web site: http://www.navh.org
E-mail: staff@navh.org
This organization concentrates on teaching people worldwide
the difference between vision impairment and blindness. The
NAVH helps people with low vision as well as their friends
and families to understand their condition and adapt to life
with low vision. The Web site includes an on-line catalog of
vision-assistance products and information on the NAVH's
large-print mail-order library.

National Association of Professional Organizers
P.O. Box 140647
Austin, TX 78714-0647
(512) 206-0151
Web site: http://www.napo.net
E-mail: napo@assnmgmt.com
This organization provides referrals to a professional organizer
in your area who can help you to plan strategies for organiz-
ing your home and your belongings, develop or improve time-
management skills, and keep track of paperwork, bills, and
other documents.

National Cancer Institute
Office of Cancer Communications
31 Center Drive, MSC 2580
Bethesda, MD 20892-2580
(800) 4-CANCER (422-6237)
Web site: http://www.cancernet.nci.nih.gov
A good source of information on cancer, including cancers
affecting vision.

National Eye Health Education Program
National Eye Institute

2020 Vision Place
Bethesda, MD 20892-3655
(301) 496-5248
Web site: http://www.nei.nih.gov/nehep
This site offers many personal stories about coping with low
vision and includes photographs illustrating what a scene
looks like to people with various forms of visual impairment.

National Federation of the Blind
1800 Johnson Street
Baltimore, MD 21230
(410) 659-9314
Web site: http://www.nfb.org
The NFB describes itself as "the nation's largest and most
influential membership organization of blind persons," with
members in all fifty states plus Washington, DC, and Puerto
Rico. The Web site includes a large amount of information for
blind people and their families, including a job referral network, a scholarship program, and information on legislation
pertaining to the blind.

National Organization for Albinism and Hypopigmentation
P.O. Box 959
East Hampstead, NH 03826-0959
(800) 473-2310
Web site: http://www.albinism.org
A volunteer organization for persons and families involved
with the condition of albinism. The Web site includes a section on driving with low vision, including a list of states that
allow people with low vision to use bioptic lenses to obtain
their driver's licenses.

Perkins School for the Blind
175 North Beacon Street

Watertown, MA 02472-2790
(617) 924-3434
Web site: http://www.perkins.pvt.k12.ma.us
This was the first school in the country founded to teach blind
people. Helen Keller's teacher, Anne Sullivan, was trained at
Perkins, and Keller herself attended the school after spending
two years in preparatory private tutoring with Sullivan. Howe
Press, which developed and sells the Perkins Brailler, and the
Perkins Braille and Talking Book Library are also a part of the
Perkins School.

Prevent Blindness America (formerly National Society to
Prevent Blindness)
500 East Remington Road
Suite 200
Schaumburg, IL 60173
(800) 331-2020
Web site: http://www.prevent-blindness.org
E-mail: info@preventblindness.org
This organization works to eliminate preventable blindness. Its
Web site offers information on ways to prevent eye injury and
how to choose proper eye protection for various activities, and
includes on-line vision tests.

The Seeing Eye, Inc.
P.O. Box 375
Morristown, NJ 07963-0375
(973) 539-4425
Web site: http://www.seeingeye.org
This organization was founded in 1929 and provides guide
dogs for visually impaired people. Its mission is "to enhance
the independence, dignity, and self-confidence of blind people
through the use of Seeing Eye dogs."

In Canada

Acting Living Alliance for Canadians with a Disability
720 Belfast Road
Suite 104
Ottawa, ON K1G 0Z5
(800) 771-0663
Web site: http://www.ala.ca
E-mail: info@ala.ca
This organization promotes inclusion and active living for
Canadians with disabilities.

Canadian National Institute for the Blind
1929 Bayview Avenue
Suite 9000
Toronto, ON M4G 3E8
(416) 234-9795
Web site: http://www.cnib.ca
The CNIB emphasizes the importance of independence for
blind and visually impaired people.

Council of Canadians with Disabilities
926-294 Portage Avenue
Winnipeg, MB R3C 0B9
(204) 947-0303
Web site: http://www.pcs.mb.ca/~ccd
E-mail: ccd@pcs.mb.ca
This organization provides a way for people with disabilities
to speak out for the rights of the disabled.

Foundation Fighting Blindness—Canada
36 Toronto Street
Suite 910
Toronto, ON M5C 2C5

(800) 461-3331
Web site: http://www.rpresearch.ca
E-mail: info@rpresearch.ca
This organization states that its goal is "to promote and support research directed to finding the cause, developing a treatment and ultimately a cure, for RP and related retinal degenerations, including macular degeneration and Usher syndrome."

Leader Dogs for the Blind
230 Strabane Avenue
Lions Manor #919
Windsor, ON N8Y 4V2
Web site: http://www.leaderdog.org
This organization provides dog guides and training for the legally blind.

For Further Reading

Alexander, Sally Hobart. *Do You Remember the Color Blue? And Other Questions Kids Ask about Blindness.* New York: Viking, 2000.

Asimov, Isaac. *Why Do Some People Wear Glasses?* Milwaukee: Gareth Stevens, 1993.

Ballard, Carol. *How Do Our Eyes See?* Chatham, NJ: Raintree Steck-Vaughn, 1998.

D'Alonzo, Thomas L. *Your Eyes! A Comprehensive Look at the Understanding and Treatment of Vision Problems.* Clifton Heights, PA: Avanti, 1991.

De Becker, Gavin. *The Gift of Fear.* Boston: Little, Brown & Co., 1997.

Goldstein, Margaret J. *Eyeglasses.* Minneapolis: Carolrhoda, 1996.

Jernigan, Kenneth, (ed.). *What You Should Know about Blindness, Services for the Blind, and the Organized Blind Movement.* Baltimore, MD: National Federation of the Blind, 1992.

Keller, Helen. *The Story of My Life.* New York: Doubleday, 1991.

National Institutes of Health. *Clinical Trials in Vision Research: Information for Patients.* Bethesda, MD: National Eye Institute, 1999.

Pringle, Laurence P. *Sight.* New York: Benchmark, 1999.

Seeing a Future: Coming to Terms with Sight Loss. London: Royal National Institute for the Blind, 1997.

Westcott, Patsy. *Living with Blindness.* Austin, TX: Raintree Steck-Vaughn, 1999.

Index